A LIVING JEWEL

16 Nov 95

Dana,

All the best to you!

Bob

A LIVING JEWEL

A BEGINNERS GUIDE TO SALT WATER AQUARIUMS

ROBERT L. FUQUA

DRAGONFLY PRODUCTIONS

4505 LINTHICUM ROAD
DAYTON, MARYLAND 21036

A LIVING JEWEL

A BEGINNERS GUIDE TO SALTWATER AQUARIUMS

ROBERT L. FUQUA

Published By:
DRAGONFLY PRODUCTIONS
4505 LINTHICUM ROAD
DAYTON, MARYLAND 21036

Copyright © 1995 by Robert L. Fuqua
All rights reserved.

PRINTED IN THE UNITED STATES
FIRST EDITION

Publisher's Cataloging in Publication Data
Fuqua, Robert L.
A Living Jewel: A Beginners Guide To Saltwater Aquariums.
Includes index.
1. Aquariums - Salt water, marine.
2. Fish - Salt water, marine.
3. Invertebrates - Salt water, marine.
4. Diseases - Salt water, marine.
SF457.1.F8   639.34   LCCCN: 95-70184
ISBN 0-9640621-0-0: $10.00 Softcover

TABLE OF CONTENTS

1	A Living Jewel	1
2	The Marine Environment	5
3	Tanks	7
4	Stands	15
5	Substrate	19
6	Salt Water	27
7	Water Circulation	35
8	Filtration	39
9	Lights	57
10	Temperature	63
11	Other Equipment	67
12	Setting Up The Aquarium	69
13	Feeding The Fish	79
14	Maintaining The Aquarium	85
15	Marine Fish	95
16	Invertebrates	159
17	Marine Fish Diseases	173
18	Introduction To Mini-Reefs	187
	Index	193
	About The Author	201

A Living Jewel

LIST OF TABLES

1	Typical tank sizes.	11
2	Principle salts found in sea water in descending order of concentration.	27
3	Relationship between temperature, specific gravity, and salinity.	29
4	Acceptable and unhealthy ranges of ammonia, nitrite and nitrate in a marine aquarium.	86

LIST OF FIGURES

1	An external filter tank.	41
2	Typical external canister filter.	43
3	Typical counter current protein skimmer.	46
4	The nitrogen cycle.	49
5	An undergravel filter.	51
6	Typical wet/dry filter.	53
7	Surface skimmer for a wet/dry filter.	54
8	A pump discharge arrangement to prevent reverse siphon action.	56
9	Siphon tube for cleaning the bottom substrate.	89
10	The basic anatomy of a fish.	96

A Living Jewel

LIST OF FISH & INVERTEBRATE ILLUSTRTIONS

Flame Angelfish	97
Batfish	101
Bicolor Blenny	103
Copper-band Butterflyfish	105
Pajama Cardinalfish	109
Percula Clown	111
Domino Damsel	115
Long-nosed Filefish	119
Yellow Goby	121
Royal Gramma	123
Arc Eye Hawkfish	125
Yellow-headed Jawfish	127
Lionfish	129
Mandarinfish	133
Moorish Idol	135
Snowflake Moray	137
Spiney Boxfish	139
Flash-back Gramma	141
Black-saddled Puffer	143
Florida Seahorse	145
Yellow Tang	147
Picasso Trigger	151
Cleaner Wrasse	155
Red Hermit Crab	161
Purple Spiny Lobster	163
Rock-boring Urchin	165
Banded-coral Shrimp	167
Comet Sea Star	171

A Living Jewel

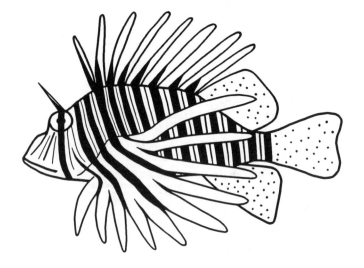

Chapter 1

A LIVING JEWEL

A well set up and maintained saltwater aquarium is beautiful, vibrant, full of life, and truly a living jewel. It is a source of constant joy and a mesmerizing focus that can lead to great relaxation. All the stresses of daily existence simply drain away as you concentrate on the life in your aquarium.

With a little knowledge, it is easy to set up and take care of a saltwater aquarium. Most people are surprised to hear this and find it hard to believe that they could actually do it themselves. This is because they have heard so many stories told by people who tried and failed to keep one going. The reason so many people have problems is that they forged into the project without a proper understanding of what they were doing. They wasted their hard earned money on equipment they did not need or was not suited for their purposes. They added too many fish to the aquarium too fast and did not feed them properly. Finally, they neglected routine aquarium cleanings and did not maintain proper water quality. In short, the poor fish never had a chance and the potential aquarist gave up in frustration.

These problems can be avoided with a little study and thought and that is exactly what this book is about. This book will guide you step by step through everything you need to know to successfully keep a saltwater aquarium. As you

A Living Jewel

read you will gain an understanding of the physical and chemical processes that are going on in the aquarium. You will also learn about the various electrical and mechanical devices that are used, and, of course, the fish. There is no need to have any advanced knowledge or specialized background, everything will be explained in easy to understand terms and concepts. If you follow these steps closely you too will be rewarded with all of the great pleasures that a saltwater aquarium has to offer.

Once you understand the information presented in this book you may want to gain an even deeper understanding of the chemistry and physics behind successful saltwater aquariums. If this is the case, you will want to continue reading and studying these subjects. This book will provide you with enough basic understanding and insight so that the more advanced books will be meaningful to you. Increasing your knowledge will only benefit you and your fish so continue to read books and magazines on these subjects and learn all you can.

Now, think about everything that you need to live a healthy, happy life. Just to stay alive you need plenty of good, clean, food and water. You also need shelter that protects you from predators and the elements. You could live in a cave by a river with plenty of fruit trees nearby, all in a nice, warm climate. These things will keep you alive but they may not necessarily keep you well and happy. You may need a better quality of life. Perhaps you need more exercise than you get from a short walk to the river or to the fruit trees. What if you want to walk to the other side of the mountain?

A Living Jewel

How will you stay safe from predators and other hazards? What if you are terribly lonely and want the companionship of another human? What if you have a companion that you absolutely cannot stand or who is hostile toward you? What if an unlimited supply of fruit does not meet all of your nutritional needs - what else will you eat? What if you become sick or injured - how will you get well again? Suppose you were not fortunate enough to live in a cave by a river and instead were locked in a small, cold, dirty, room and only fed bread and water? Consider the fish in your aquarium. Are they happy in the fish equivalent of a nice tropical setting with friendly companions and plenty of good food to eat or are they locked in a cold, tiny cell and fed a poor diet? The fish in our aquariums have needs just as you and I do. Since the fish have been removed form their natural environment and are now in our aquariums, it is our responsibility to satisfy their needs and provide them with the necessary care. If we do not, our fish die unnecessarily in ugly, polluted tanks because of our negligence.

My whole philosophy on keeping saltwater fish is to duplicate their natural environment as closely as possible. This means that you must choose your fish carefully and understand the conditions they need in order to live happy, healthy lives. For example; what temperature, salinity and pH do they require? What kind of shelter and hiding places do they need? What foods do they eat? Are they aggressive or timid around other fish of the same or different species? How sensitive are they to water quality? The more we know the answers to these questions and are able to duplicate these conditions, the better off our fish will be. The purpose of this

A Living Jewel

book is to help you gain the information you need in a concise, straight forward manner. As your aquarium flourishes and becomes more beautiful you will begin to see that it really is a living jewel.

Chapter 2

THE MARINE ENVIRONMENT

In order for the fish and other inhabitants of our saltwater aquarium to be happy and healthy we must duplicate their preferred environment as closely as possible. To do this it is necessary to understand the marine environment that they came from. Since most of our aquariums are the new homes for fish that came from a coral reef, this is the environment we will concentrate on.

To start with, we need to list the various conditions that describe a coral reef. The first thing we notice is that there is an abundance of sunshine and that the air and water are warm. As we enter the water we see that it is in constant motion due to wave action, surges, tides, and currents. We also note that there is virtually no organic debris. Everything from feces to dead fish is processed by the water and the various life forms and reduced to harmless substances. Everything is either consumed or recycled. Although many plants and animals live on and around the reef, it is not overcrowded and each life form has adequate space to live in. Each life form performs functions that are vital to the survivability of the reef. These include scavengers that eat sick and dying animals, filter feeders that help clean the water of organic debris, and herbivores that help control algae growth. Finally, when observed from season to season and year to year, the conditions on a healthy reef either remain constant

The Marine Environment

or change very slowly. Only when outside forces are applied such as massive oil spills, silt, and chemical runoff from the land, and ships running aground, do the conditions on the reef change quickly and they always change for the worse.

The above described conditions are those of a perfectly balanced ecological system. The more closely we can duplicate these conditions the better off the inhabitants of our aquarium will be. Realistically we will never be able to recreate everything perfectly. So, many functions of the various reef inhabitants and other natural chemical reactions have to be duplicated by electrical, mechanical, and chemical means as well as by human intervention. For example, we set up lights to mimic the solar spectrum and the day-night cycle. We set up filtration systems that combine mechanical, chemical, and biological filtration to maintain high water quality. We add heaters to maintain warm temperatures and we manually clean the tank of organic debris that has settled to the bottom and into the nooks and crannies of the rocks and decorations. If we have a sick or dying fish, we will remove it to another tank for treatment. If we find a dead fish, we remove it as well. Of course, we also feed our fish a proper diet. Only through a combination of the proper equipment and our intervention are we able to maintain our aquariums in as close to natural conditions as possible. The rest of this book will describe all of the necessary equipment and actions that we must take to maintain a salt water aquarium successfully.

Chapter 3

TANKS

We now have a basic understanding of the marine environment and our responsibility to mimic it as closely as possible. The next step is to start learning about the various equipments and techniques that are needed and how they all function.

The most obviously needed piece of equipment is the tank. The primary function of a tank is to serve as a leak free container to hold the water that our fish will live in. It must be clean and free of pollutants and durable so that it is serviceable for many years. It is also necessary that at least one side be transparent so that we can see into the tank to enjoy our fish and to help us keep it properly maintained. Finally, the tank should be pleasing to look at especially if it will be located in an area where many people will see it.

People have been keeping fish alive in some kind of container for enjoyment, study, consumption, or other uses throughout history. A wide variety of materials such as, ceramics, wood, metal, cement, fiberglass, plastics, stone and glass (or a combination of these materials) have been used to make tanks. These tanks have been made in numerous sizes and shapes from small bowls to huge rectangular vessels. Modern mass production techniques combined with high quality materials and durable sealants have given us a wide variety of affordable tanks in both standard and custom sizes and shapes. Glass and acrylic have emerged as the most common materials used in modern tanks. Each of these materials have advantages and disadvantages and the one best suited for your aquarium depends on your specific requirements and goals. The pros and cons of both glass and acrylic tanks are discussed below to help you make the proper decision.

Glass tanks

The most common type of tank uses glass for the four sides and bottom. These tanks are strong and durable and perform quite well in almost any application. Originally, glass tanks were constructed by cementing the five glass pieces (some early tanks had a slate bottom instead of glass) into a metal framework. This framework extended along all four sides of the top and bottom as well as all four corners where the glass walls connected providing strength and protecting the glass from damage. Although the frame served a noble function it was not always nice to look at, it was subject to corrosion, and it blocked part of the view of the inhabitants.

With the development of a very good construction adhesive and sealant called silicone rubber it became possible to construct a tank without a metal framework resulting in minimal visual obstruction. A plastic framework was placed around the top and bottom of the tank providing strength, durability, and convenient mounting points for lights and accessories. This framework also came with different finishes adding to the overall attractiveness of the tank. Today virtually all glass tanks are constructed using this technique.

Tanks

The major disadvantage of glass is that the larger tanks are very heavy. This weight, combined with a high center of gravity and large size, make large glass tanks extremely awkward to move and carry. A thirty gallon tank is about the limit for one person to move so ask someone for help when moving larger tanks.

Acrylic tanks
Acrylic tanks have become increasingly popular over the last few years. These tanks are usually made out of four pieces, the bottom, top, back, and one piece with two corners that serves as the front and two sides. These pieces are joined with acrylic cement and no other special sealants are needed. One of the first things that you will notice about these tanks is their clarity and virtually unobstructed view. They make particularly striking additions to any home. An additional nice feature is their light weight and a fifty gallon tank can be moved and carried by one person without too much difficulty.

The key disadvantage to acrylic tanks is that the material is very soft and can be easily scratched. It is very important to take great care when moving or cleaning these tanks so that they do not get nicked or scratched. Always use a soft cloth when cleaning the inside or outside of an acrylic tank. To use anything more abrasive will result in fine scratches or hazing of the surface. You also need to evaluate the location of the tank and the possibility for potential harm. Active children, misguided vacuum cleaner wands, etc., can mark an acrylic tank for life. While it may be possible to polish out these scratch marks, the results are never perfect. These

Tanks

tanks have an additional disadvantage in that they are more expensive than a glass tank.

Tank sizes and styles

Tanks are available in a wide variety of gallon sizes such as 1, 2.5, 5, 10, 15, 20, 29, 30, 50, 55, 65, 70, 75, 90, 100, 135, 150 and on up. There are two common styles: one is the standard size and the other has the same length and width but is taller. Many other sizes can also be found. Table 1 provides a comparison of common tank sizes. If you have specific needs it is possible to have a custom tank made. The standard size tanks are the best buy because they are readily available, use standard size accessories (lights), and are much cheaper than custom tanks. While it is possible to successfully operate small salt water aquariums of ten gallons or less, tanks of thirty gallons or larger are recommended because they provide more room for the fish and it is easier to maintain a proper chemical balance.

The traditional tank is shaped as a rectangle. Because of the use of modern materials and improved construction techniques it is now possible to also make tanks in a variety of shapes such as hexagon, octagon, towers, and even cylindrical. These shapes can make it possible to establish a salt water aquarium in rooms where a standard rectangular tank would not fit well.

Tanks can also be purchased with additional features such as background colors or scenery. The primary purpose of these is to provide a more pleasing view by hiding the filters, wires and tubes that hang off the back of the tank.

Tanks

The secondary purpose is to enhance the scenery in the tank. Their are two types of background. The first is a solid colored back usually in light blue or black. This is very attractive and does a good job of dressing up the aquarium. The black background gives the tank a classic, dramatic look but can also make the tank look less bright and the fish somewhat harder to see. The blue background adds light and makes everything show up better, but may not match the decor of the rest of the room very well. The second type of background is usually a piece of thin material that hangs on the outside of the tank. The most common design of this background is a reef picture. Sometimes the material will have a crystallized or crazed design in a variety of colors.

size gallons	long	wide	high	style
	----------inches---------			
5	16	8	10	standard
10	20	10	12	standard
20	30	12	12	standard
20	24	12	16	tall
30	36	13	16	standard
30	24	12	24	tall
50	36	18	18	standard
55	48	13	20	standard
70	48	18	20	standard
100	72	18	18	standard
135	72	18	24	standard
150	72	18	28	standard

Table 1. Typical tank sizes.

Tanks

Used tanks

You can find lots of used tanks at garage sales and flea markets. If you find one that you like check it carefully for chips, scratches, cracks and evidence of leaks. Ask the owner if the tank is guaranteed not to leak. Small leaks can usually be fixed with an application of silicone rubber and this is important to keep in mind. Good tanks can be found at reasonable prices, so if money is a concern a used tank is a viable option. Be sure that you are familiar with the cost of a new tank of the same size so that you can accurately compare prices.

Selecting a tank

The glass tanks are heavier, and the larger ones will require one or more people to help you place it where you want. The acrylic tanks are very good looking but great care must be taken to avoid scratching them and damaging their good looks. Glass and acrylic are different from each other and neither is inherently better or worse than the other. Both will serve you well. It is up to you to make a choice based on the pros and cons of each and your own personal preference and circumstances.

Selecting which size of tank to purchase also depends on several other factors. The room you have available for it, your budget, and how many fish you want to keep. If you have to purchase a smaller tank than you really want you may have to fight the temptation to put too many fish in it. The number of fish you can keep depends on how many gallons of water the tank holds and how much surface area of water is exposed to the air for a proper gas exchange. A tall

Tanks

tank with a small surface area exposed to the air will accommodate fewer fish than a tank containing the same number of gallons but with a larger exposed surface area. Since too many fish can overburden your filter system, pollute the tank and cause the fish to become ill and die, it is important to be conservative. Chapter 12, Setting Up The Aquarium, will discuss how many fish can be kept in an aquarium. Remember, we want our fish to be happy and healthy so an uncrowded aquarium is important.

So, you have many choices to make before you purchase your tank. Start by considering which room the aquarium will occupy. Determine how much space you have available both horizontally and vertically. Do not forget the filter and other items that may be hanging off the back of the tank to make sure that you have enough room in front of the wall. Also consider where your power outlets are placed so that you can avoid using extension cords. If you must use an extension cord, it is much better to use a power strip that is designed to safely provide power to several devices. Also consider how many fish you want to keep and how many rocks you will provide for decoration and hiding places. The best prices for new tanks can usually be found at the larger "high volume" aquarium shops, however, great bargains can also be found at some smaller shops. Additionally, if you want an acrylic tank or a tank with non-standard sizes, be prepared to pay more than you would for a standard glass tank. If money is a consideration, take the extra time to check prices from several locations and visit garage sales to make sure that you are getting the most for your hard earned money.

Tanks

Now decide what, if any, kind of background you want. If you want a solid color background but cannot find a tank with that available, it is possible to paint it yourself using a glossy enamel spray paint and carefully masking off the other surfaces of the tank. If you want one of the other backgrounds be sure to apply it before the tank is on the stand and full of water.

Chapter 4

STANDS

The next major consideration is what kind of stand to use. Stands serve three basic purposes. First, they must safely hold the weight of your tank and water. Second, they must allow for easy access to your tank and third, they should be pleasing to look at.

Weight of the aquarium and water

Salt water weighs about 8.5 pounds per gallon and this can add up to a lot of weight when bigger tanks are filled. As an example, the water in my 150-gallon tank weighs 1275 pounds, so obviously a strong stand is required to adequately support this weight. When bigger tanks are used it is also very important to consider the total weight that the floor must support. Consider again my 150-gallon tank sitting in a wooden stand with a large wet/dry filter and a wooden canopy over the lights. By adding 1275 pounds for the water, 200 pounds for the tank, 150 pounds for the stand and canopy, and another 100 pounds for the filter, lights, accessories, rocks and decorations, we arrive at a total weight of 1725 pounds or almost one ton! Any time your actual aquarium load approaches 1000 pounds or greater you should consider using additional support under the floor. For this tank I use two floor jacks in the basement to support the weight of the 150-gallon aquarium on the first floor. Some buildings are stronger or weaker than others so consider the overall condition and strength of the building and exactly where you want to place your aquarium when deciding if any additional support is necessary. If you are in doubt, consult with a reputable construction company or your local building codes to be sure. I do not want to scare you about the weight of your tank but you do need to be cautious. If this weight is not properly supported the stress could cause cracks in the walls, a bowed floor, or worse.

Wrought iron stands

In the past, the most common type of stand was an open wrought iron framework painted black. These were strong, rugged and had the added advantage of being able to hold a second aquarium, books, plants, or accessories in a shelf area on the bottom. These stands are still available and do a very good job however they are somewhat rustic looking and may not fit into the decor of your room.

Wooden stands

Wooden stands are becoming more popular. Many of them have a shelf on the bottom to hold another tank, plants, or other items and some even have the bottom enclosed with doors to provide a nice out-of-sight storage area. Some wooden stands even come in kit form that you assemble making them easier to bring home or move. Many new wooden stands have a very finished look, so that they fit in very well with your other furniture.

Other stands

Bricks or cement blocks and boards can also be used, especially if you are on a tight budget. This approach de-

Stands

serves a few words of caution. Be sure that the surface that the aquarium will sit on is flat and level. Otherwise the tank may be subjected to twisting forces that can cause leaks or even break the glass. Also be careful about how high you stack the bricks or cement blocks so that the structure is solid and will not wobble.

One of the most stunning ways to display your aquarium is to build it into a wall. As always, proper support is essential not only for the tank but also for the wall with the new hole in it. This approach also requires extra space behind the aquarium so that you can have access to the tank for set up and maintenance.

Purchasing a stand

Wrought iron and wooden stands can be purchased new at most aquarium shops. They can also be found at garage sales or flea markets. There are two concerns when buying a used stand: is it in good condition, and is the price reasonable? Closely examine the stand from all angles to include the bottom. Remember that an aquarium full of water is very heavy, so you are looking for any sign of weakness such as cracks or loose joints. A good test is to try to twist the stand by pulling on one side and pushing on the other while observing the joints and sides. A good stand will not give and will feel like one solid piece. If you do detect some give check further for any loose nuts/bolts or other hardware. If the looseness can be corrected by tightening the hardware, the stand may be acceptable. If not, it is probably not worth considering. No one wants to have dead fish and fifty gallons of salt water all over the carpet because a shaky stand

Stands

was purchased to save a few dollars.

During the life of any salt water aquarium, saltwater will be spilled, dripped, or sprayed onto the stand and the surrounding surfaces. Salt water is very corrosive and if it is not cleaned up it can attack the wood or metal and create problems. So, check thoroughly for any evidence of corrosion. Simple surface salt or light surface rust is probably acceptable provided that you can clean it up and repaint if necessary. However, if the corrosion is any more severe than that, it is better to find a stand somewhere else. The final concern is the price. Before you go looking for a used stand, know the price of a new one. This allows you to avoid paying full price for a shaky stand that you will have to spend more time and money on to make it serviceable.

Both the wooden and the iron stand are good choices. If you have less money to spend, bricks or cement blocks and boards are acceptable. If money is no object, you can go top of the line and have your tank built into a wall. The stand you choose depends on your budget, your room, and the look that you wish to achieve.

Chapter 5

SUBSTRATE

For purposes of saltwater aquariums, the substrate is any hard surface that can serve as a location for microscopic and macroscopic life to live on. This includes the sides of the tank, the rocks and decorations, and the material that covers the bottom. This chapter will focus on the layer of material placed on the bottom of the aquarium. The bottom substrate has two functions: it improves the looks of the bottom of the aquarium and it provides a surface for bacteria live on. This bacteria is useful in reducing organic waste and the ammonia that the fish excrete to less harmful substances. This process will be more thoroughly discussed in Chapter 8, Filtration. The remainder of this chapter will discuss the various kinds of substrate and how they perform in an aquarium.

The type and amount of bottom substrate you need depends on whether you use an undergravel filter. Specifics of undergravel filters will be discussed in Chapter 8, Filtration; however, the substrate requirements for this type of filter will be addressed at the end of this chapter as well.

How the substrate functions
For now we must gain an understanding of how the bottom substrate functions. In a well filtered aquarium, most of the uneaten food and the waste that the fish excrete will be collected and processed by the filter. However, a portion of

Substrate

this organic deris will always fall to the bottom of the aquarium. If this debris is allowed to remain there, it will decay and become a source of pollution for your aquarium. If this developing condition is not rectified, the water in your aquarium will become hopelessly fouled and poison your fish.

A layer of bottom substrate several inches thick with grains larger than one eighth of an inch in diameter will allow excess waste and debris to accumulate. So, the first thing we realize is that a very fine substrate with grains of one eighth inch or smaller is required. Even with a small grained substrate, minute particles of organic debris will eventually accumulate and permeate the depth of the substrate. You may not see it and your aquarium may look great, but all is not well. To test the condition of the bottom substrate, stir a section to see how much organic waste clouds the water. If you see any clouds of waste you know that the substrate is accumulating organic debris that needs to be cleaned. Our ultimate goal is to keep the aquarium as free of organic debris as possible, and allowing it to build up in a thick substrate is counter to this goal. So, the next thing we realize is that a thinner layer of substrate will contain less debris than a thicker one and will be easier to clean.

Thickness of the substrate

There is really no need to have a bottom substrate deeper than one half inch unless you are using an undergravel filter or if you have fish, such as the jawfish, that require deep bottom substrates in which to build their home. If you absolutely must have a substrate that is several inches thick you must commit yourself to a weekly ritual of cleaning all

Substrate

of the waste and debris, so that it does not pollute the aquarium. You will probably tire of this extra work or at least miss a week occasionally and your fish will suffer for it. The best thing to do is to design your aquarium so that it requires a minimum amount of maintenance. This makes the keeping of an aquarium more enjoyable for you; the aquarium will always look great, and most important of all, the fish will be healthier and happier. In short, everyone benefits.

Most aquarium books recommend several inches of substrate for decoration and biological filtration, and you may now be confused over how much to use. While it is true that some biological filtration will take place at all depths of the substrate, it is not complete filtration and will not keep up with the organic waste that is constantly accumulating. A thin layer of substrate is much better because it allows for some biological filtration to take place, and avoids the problem of accumulated waste. Furthermore, one-half inch or less of substrate is far easier to clean than several inches making it easier for you to keep your aquarium pristine. If you are still not sure, consider this. What happens if your power goes off for an extended time and you lose all water circulation and filtration? Do you want your aquarium to go through this stressful period starting with nice, pristine conditions or do you want it to start with several inches of accumulated organic debris sitting on the bottom? I believe that we must give our aquariums every chance for success possible. Accumulated organic waste in the bottom is a problem waiting to happen, and it is a problem that can easily be avoided.

Substrate

How much substrate to acquire

To determine how much substrate you need to acquire, find the area of your tank bottom in square inches by multiplying the length of your aquarium by the width. Next multiply this number by the depth in inches of substrate you plan to use. This will give you the volume of substrate required in cubic inches. For example, if you have a 55-gallon tank with a bottom that is 48 by 13 inches, you have an area of 624 square inches. Now, if you want a substrate that is one quarter of an inch deep, multiply 624 square inches by .25 inches to get 156 cubic inches. A bag that is 6 by 13 by 2 inches would give you exactly 156 cubic inches of substrate.

Beach sand

It is time to move on to the specific types of substrate and discuss the good and bad points of each. The most common kind of substrate in use is beach silica sand. If you live near a nice clean beach you can collect your own or you can buy sand in any aquarium shop. Of the various sizes available, it is best to use a fine sand that has particles no larger than one eighth of an inch in diameter. Larger grains of sand will allow particles of organic debris to become trapped as described above. The silica in the sand can also contribute to the growth of brown diatom algae in your aquarium, which can be a nuisance.

Crushed coral sand

If you have ever had the wonderful opportunity to snorkel or SCUBA dive on a coral reef, you may have noticed that the bottom of the ocean there is covered with crushed coral sand. The parrot fish is a very common reef inhabitant

Substrate

that has a sharp parrot like beak and beautiful iridescent scales, thus it is aptly named. One of their favorite foods is the coral polyp. The parrot fish bites off small pieces of the coral formation, ingests the polyps and excretes the hard stony parts as coral sand. This coral sand can be collected at the reef or purchased at an aquarium shop. It is just as desirable as beach silica sand and has the additional property of being able to release calcium back into the salt water to help maintain proper chemical balances. Coral sand is preferable in a mini-reef aquarium.

Colored sand
You will probably find colored sand at your pet shop and may want to use it to make your aquarium more colorful. While this sand may be very attractive, it is artificially colored. Since the salt water environment is very harsh and corrosive, it may leach the chemicals and dyes out of the sand to the detriment of your fish.

Glass
You may be tempted to use colored glass that has been tumbled to make it smooth. This is a much safer way to add colors to your aquarium bottom, but remember that a large sized substrate leaves room for the accumulation of debris that is bad for your aquarium. Some people may want to use marbles for their unique effect; however, these are not good at all because the large space that exists between them allows organic debris to accumulate.

Cleaning the substrate
Before you use it, thoroughly wash the substrate ma-

Substrate

terial to remove any dirt, dust, and organic debris. Even if the bag says that it is pre-cleaned, you should wash it again to make sure. Often during transit the material can get crushed against itself and make additional dust that you do not want in your aquarium. The best method to use to wash the material is to spread some of it out over a fine mesh screen (finer than your smallest grains) and spray it thoroughly with a garden hose until the runoff water is clear. Continue doing this until all of it is clean. If you do not have any fine screen, you can wash it with a bucket and a hose. Fill a bucket half full or less with the material and force the hose down into it with the water running. Stir the material with your hands and the hose to flush out any debris and dirt. Continue this process until all of the substrate material is clean.

Rock and coral

In addition to your bottom substrate, it is also a good idea to add rocks or chunks of coral to your aquarium. These items serve several purposes. First they enhance the looks of your aquarium. Secondly they provide more surface area for biological filtration. Thirdly, and more importantly, they provide hiding places for your fish to retreat to for rest and safety. After a rough day we all look forward to getting home (or even just to our cars) so we can relax and unwind. Fish also need some special place to retreat to. The best rocks to use are six or more inches across and have a rough shape with lots of big nooks and holes for the fish to hide in and swim through. Yes, it is true that these nooks and holes are areas that debris can accumulate in. However, I believe that providing hiding places for the fish is more important. Any accumulated debris can be removed by siphoning it out of these

Substrate

areas during cleaning. Siphoning will be discussed further in Chapter 14, Maintaining The Aquarium.

If you want to use coral pieces either collect the big chunks that wash up on the beach or buy the big rough chunks that someone else collected off the beach. Do not buy the beautiful and fragile coral heads that are for sale. Most of these corals are harvested live, then killed and bleached to be sold in stores. While these are very attractive in an aquarium, their proper place is alive in the ocean. Coral is an endangered species and we do not want to encourage anyone to harvest it and kill it buy giving them money to do so. It is also important that you do not collect and kill the coral yourself. Some advanced aquarists will collect or buy live coral to nurture and keep alive in their mini-reefs. This is different and acceptable provided the aquarist has the specialized knowledge and equipment to keep the coral alive and healthy. Above all, it is important that the living coral is not destroyed.

Substrate

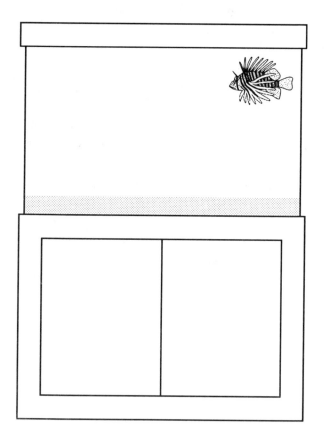

Chapter 6

SALT WATER

The key difference between salt water and fresh water is the chemical content of the water. This chapter will discuss the chemistry and properties of salt water in detail.

Composition of salt water

Salt water is different from fresh water because of the types and amounts of chemicals that are dissolved in it. Fresh water weighs about 8.3 pounds per gallon and salt water weighs about 8.5 pounds. The extra .2 pounds in a gallon of salt water is due to the dissolved chemicals. Table 2 lists the principle salts found in sea water in descending order of concentration.

Sodium Chloride	$NaCl$
Magnesium Chloride	$MgCl_2$
Magnesium Sulfate	$MgSO_4$
Calcium Sulfate	$NaSO_4$
Potassium Sulfate	K_2SO_4
Calcium Carbonate	$CaCO_3$
Calcium or Sodium Bromide	KBr or $NaBr$

Table 2. Principle salts found in sea water in descending order of concentration.

Salt Water

In addition, every other element on earth will be found dissolved in salt water in minute quantities and these are referred to as trace elements. All natural salt water world wide contains these principal salts in the same proportions. The trace elements however, will be found at different concentrations and proportions. Saltwater fish require the presence of these principal salts as well as many of the trace elements in order to survive. That is to say that they have a physiological dependence on salt water and can not live indefinitely in fresh water.

Salinity
The overall concentration of all of these salts in the water is referred to as salinity. Concentrations of chemicals in salt water are measured in parts per thousand and expressed as ppt or by the symbol o/oo. The surface of the earth is approximately 70% water and all of the world's oceans contain salt water. However, factors such as fresh water run-off from the land, geological confinement, and lack of global mixing have resulted in each of the oceans having a slightly different salinity than the rest. Remember that the relative proportion of each of the principal salts remains the same; however, the overall percentage of all of the dissolved salts in the water is different. For example, the Red Sea has a salinity of 40 o/oo, the Pacific Ocean is 35.5 o/oo, the Atlantic Ocean is 37 o/oo and the Indian Ocean ranges between 30-34 o/oo. The average salinity world wide is 35 o/oo.

Specific gravity
In addition to the salinity increasing as salts and trace elements are dissolved in water, the specific gravity (also

Salt Water

known as density) of the resultant salt water also increases. Specific gravity is the ratio of the mass of salt water to an equal mass of fresh water. Since salt water has more mass than fresh water, the ratio of these two numbers will always be greater than one. As temperature rises, water volume increases slightly, and, as a result, specific gravity and salinity change with temperature. To be absolutely precise, we must always specify temperature when salinity and specific gravity measurements are made. Table 3 shows the relationship between temperature, specific gravity, and salinity over the common range of temperatures found in temperate waters world wide. For example, the specific gravity of ocean salt water with a salinity of 35 o/oo and a temperature of 70 degrees Fahrenheit is 1.025.

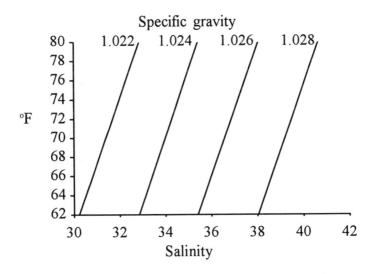

Table 3. Relationship between temperature, specific gravity, and salinity.

Salt Water

Thermometers and hydrometers

Temperature, specific gravity, and salinity conditions in our aquariums are monitored using two instruments. The first instrument is a thermometer, which is used to determine the exact temperature. The second instrument is a hydrometer, which is a floating device with calibrations for various specific gravities on it. As the specific gravity of the water increases, the hydrometer will float higher in the water and the line where the water crosses the markings is the measurement of the specific gravity of the water. When reading this measurement, it is important to know that water demonstrates a property called adhesion, which means that it will tend to "wet" the objects that it touches. That is to say, it will tend to rise up the side of the hydrometer slightly higher than the actual height of the water. When you try to read the hydrometer, you will see a line that is equal in height to the actual water level and you will also see another line on the hydrometer that is slightly higher and is the result of adhesion. The extra height caused by adhesion is referred to as the meniscus. The bottom of these two lines is used for the measurement. Now that the temperature and specific gravity are known, the salinity of the water can be determined by using Table 3. Thermometers and hydrometers can either be purchased separately or combined into one unit with the thermometer occupying the bottom float section of the hydrometer.

Since it is our goal to maintain our aquariums as close to natural reef conditions as possible, we need to determine the temperature and salinity requirements of our fish and use Table 3 to determine the specific gravity. We then adjust the

Salt Water

amount of disolved salt in our tank until the hydrometer registers the desired specific gravity. Later in this chapter we will learn more about how to raise the salinity of the water. Most marine fish that live in the coral reef environment prefer a salinity of around 34 o/oo which equates to a specific gravity of 1.024 at 78 F.

pH

Another important aspect of our salt water is the well known but little understood pH. These letters are the abbreviation for the Latin words *pondus hydrogenii* which means "power of hydrogen". This refers to the relative amounts of positively charged hydrogen ions H^+ to the negatively charged hydroxyl ions OH^-. The relationship between the hydrogen and hydroxyl ions is expressed on a logarithmic scale from 1 to 14. Each point on the scale represents a concentration that is ten times higher than the previous point. A pH of 1 represents an acid and a pH of 14 represents a base. A pH of 7 represents a neutral solution with an equal number of hydrogen and hydroxyl ions. The pH is important to marine life just as it is to us. No one or no thing wants to swim in a water solution that is either highly acidic or basic. Each animal has a pH range that they are comfortable with and can thrive in. The pH of coral reef salt water typically runs between 8.1 and 8.3 which is slightly basic and this is the range that we want our aquariums to stay in. When the pH moves beyond this range our aquarium is in serious trouble and we need to take immediate steps to correct it. This is done by water changes or the addition of chemicals.

Salt Water

Acquiring salt water

So, where do we get our salt water? If you are fortunate enough to live near a pristine, healthy, coral reef with crystal clear water you can collect your own salt water directly from the reef. When collecting natural sea water, it is best to take it from within the water column and not from the surface. This is because the surface tension of the water often causes organic debris to collect there. Do not collect natural salt water from any other source. If the water is less than crystal clear, it is probably loaded with organic and inorganic debris and should not be used. In addition, water from any other source could be contaminated by unseen chemicals from run off from the land, discharge from sewage treatment plants, or dumping of industrial waste. It is better to be super conservative when collecting natural water because the life of your fish may be at risk. Before you use any natural salt water it is always a good idea to test it for pH, ammonia, nitrite, and nitrate to make sure that it is suitable for use in your aquarium. Water testing is discussed further in Chapter 14, Maintaining The Aquarium.

If you do not have ready access to that pristine, healthy, reef, you will have to mix your own salt water. This is actually very easy because you can buy bags of instant salt water mix at any marine aquarium shop. All you have to do is add this mix to fresh water to create artificial ocean water. There are two types of mixes available. Both types contain all of the standard saltwater chemicals but one also has added vitamins. The kind with the extra vitamins is often advertised as being designed for mini-reefs but is also just fine for fish only aquariums. I prefer the type without the added vitamins

Salt Water

because of the potential of the added vitamins to increase the level of nutrients in the water, thus causing more algae growth than I want. My advise is to start with this type and then experiment with the one with added vitamins after your tank is established. Observe the water quality, algae growth, and overall health of your fish to determine which one you prefer.

As the water in your aquarium evaporates, it leaves behind the salt and causes the salinity of the tank to increase. To compensate, all you have to do is add fresh water to reduce the salinity back to the desired level. Also, over time your fish will slowly consume some of the trace elements in the salt water. To compensate for this, it is good to replace some of your salt water with an equal amount of new salt water. If you ever notice that the salinity is below the desired level, just add a concentrated mixture of salt water to the tank. But be sure to do this slowly to avoid causing undue stress on your fish due to a rapidly changing condition. More information on how to maintain your aquarium will be presented in Chapter 14, Maintaining The Aquarium.

As a final bit of advise, it is worth taking some extra time to shop around for the best price on salt water mix. The best buys are usually (but not always) found in the larger "discount" aquarium shops. However, sometimes the smaller shops wil sell salt mix at very competitive prices. Since you may encounter substantial markups on salt mix, it pays to check around before you buy.

Salt Water

Chapter 7

WATER CIRCULATION

Circulation of the water is vitally important to an aquarium for many reasons. With the water in constant motion, organic debris is more likely to be drawn into the filtration system and less likely to settle into the substrate. A good source of water circulation will also disturb the surface water allowing a thorough gaseous exchange and oxygenation of the water. Circulation allows for a complete mixing of the warm and cold areas of the tank to insure a constant uniform temperature. Additionally, if your tank has any animals that are filter feeders, such as sponges or clams, good circulation helps provide them with a continuous source of nutrition. So, you can see, good water circulation is extremely important to the well being of your fish.

How much circulation
The question now is, "how much circulation is enough?". You should try to achieve a flow rate of from three to six times your tank size in gallons each hour. As an example, for a 50-gallon tank, a water flow rate of from 150 to 300 gallons per hour is desirable. A water flow less than this can create dead spots where the debris will settle. A water flow greater than this can create currents that are too strong and can cause stress among some of your animals. As for surface disturbance, it is not necessary to set up a small tidal wave on the surface. It is good enough for the surface

Water Circulation

to have a continuous series of ripples running through it. The goal here is to avoid a flat, undisturbed, surface that can become stagnant.

Many water pumps are rated according to how many gallons per hour they can produce. If you do not know the flow rate of your pump, it is possible to determine it with a simple test. Direct the output of the pump into a gallon container and count how many seconds are needed to fill it. To convert the number of seconds it takes to fill the container to the flow rate of the pump in gallons per hour, divide 3600 by the number of seconds. For example, if it takes 10 seconds to fill the container, the flow rate is 3600 divided by 10 or 360 gallons per hour.

There are two primary methods you can use to induce water circulation and they will be discussed below. It may be necessary to use a combination of these methods to achieve proper circulation. Remember that we want both a proper mixing of the water and disturbance of the surface. Observe you tank closely to make sure that these conditions are met. If they are not, experiment with redirecting the flow to different locations or add other sources of water circulation until you achieve the desired level.

Filter outlet

The most convenient way to achieve this level of water flow is through the water return of your filter system. Some filters use a cascade water return whereby the water overflows the filter and falls back into the tank by gravity. These do a great job of disturbing the surface but typically do not

Water Circulation

have a great flow rate. Other filter systems discharge the water through a tube either close to the water surface or somewhere deeper. These systems typically have a greater flow rate but may not cause enough surface disturbance. Either system may be sufficient depending on the size of your aquarium and the individual specifications of the filter. Also, each system enhances circulation because the filter siphon tube draws water from low in the aquarium.

Auxiliary pumps

Another convenient method of improving circulation is to use small auxiliary pumps. Some of these pumps, called power heads, are designed for use with undergravel filters, but they work just fine as stand alone circulation pumps. Many of these pumps come with a variety of mounting hardware that will typically include clamps for attaching them to the top of the tank or suction cups for mounting them directly to the glass. They frequently also come with attachments that can be placed over the pump outlet to direct the water flow in different directions. Since many of them are submersible, it is possible to place them anywhere within the water column to get the circulation that you are working toward. However, remember that not all pumps are submersible, so check the specifications thoroughly to make sure that it can be operated safely underwater!

Air bubblers

Many people think that it is necessary to have air pumps and air stones providing air bubbles in the aquarium. While air pumps and bubblers may be appropriate for small freshwater aquariums, they deliver a very limited water flow

Water Circulation

rate and are not recommended for properly set up saltwater aquariums. The air bubbles also do not add significantly to the gaseous exchange during their quick trip to the surface. If the surface is already adequately disturbed by discharge from your pumps or filters, the bubbles become insignificant. The air bubbles even have a disadvantage when used in saltwater aquariums in that as they break on the surface they create a mist of salt water that dampens the outside surface of the aquarium, filters, and lights. This mist can even cause drips down the side of the aquarium and onto the stand or even down electrical wires. When the dampness dries it leaves behind a white coating of salt that can be quite a nuisance. As long as the mist continues the coating of salt will grow larger and larger. This growth is refered to as salt creep. Additionally, this salt mist can lead to corrosion of light fixtures and other metal hardware and even cause electrical hazards. So, as attractive as a stream of bubbles can be, an air pump and air stone bubbler are not worth the trouble.

Chapter 8

FILTRATION

There are two types of filtration, mechanical and biological. Mechanical filtration removes organic and inorganic debris, and unwanted chemicals from the water by passing it through various materials. Biological filtration uses biochemical means of converting harmful organic substances to less harmful substances by passing the water through colonies of bacteria living in the filter substrate. Both types of filtration are required and many filters combine them into one system.

The entire success of your aquarium depends on maintaining the water as clean and free of debris as possible. If this is not done, the excretions of your fish will build up to levels that are toxic to all living creatures in the aquarium. Additionally, other debris such as uneaten food will decay leaving behind fouled water and even more toxic substances. The level of filtration that you use will make or break your aquarium and this filtration is the one key area that you absolutely must do right. You can never have too much filtration but you can easily have too little, and the results will range from a generally unhealthy tank to complete disaster. So, this chapter is of vital importance to the success of your aquarium.

When you go into an aquarium shop, you will see a wide variety of filter systems offered for sale. They each have different features and maintenance requirements, and a person can be easily overwhelmed by all of the choices. This chapter will also describe the various features of the basic types of filtration systems so that you can make wise choices.

Mechanical filters

The first filters were mechanical, so we will start by describing them. The most basic type of mechanical filter consists of a tank that hangs off the back of your aquarium. Water is siphoned into this tank through one or more tubes that have one end in the aquarium and the other in the filter tank. A pump moves the water back into the aquarium and while the water is making this round trip it passes through the filter material. The primary filter material in use is polyester floss which is very effective at straining out debris. The filter floss can either come lose or in pre-formed inserts. Loose filter floss is purchased in bags, and you remove what you need and place it in the filter tank according to the manufacturer's instructions. If the filter uses preformed inserts, you simply pull out the old and insert the new. Very often the insert will contain both the floss and activated carbon in one convenient package. Activated carbon removes unwanted chemicals and will be discussed in detail later in this chapter. Another filter media that is widely used is polyurethane foam. These can be purchased as pre-shaped forms or as blocks that you cut to the size you need.

External tank filter

The external tank filter was one of the first to be used by salt water aquarist and is still in use today. Figure 1 shows what this filter looks like. When maintained routinely, these

Filtration

filters do a good job of filtering your aquarium. To remove the used filter floss, it is sometimes easier to remove the entire filter from the aquarium and work on it in a sink. This is an inconvenient and messy process and can become a true test of your dedication to your aquarium. One of these filters is adequate for no more than a 50-gallon tank and if you have a larger tank you need to use more than one.

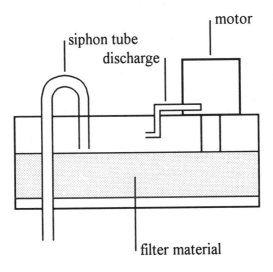

Figure 1. An external filter tank.

These filters are durable and have the added advantage that they also perform limited biological filtration. This is accomplished by leaving some old floss in the filter along with the new floss after you perform your routine cleaning. The piece of old floss provides a colony of beneficial bacteria that will propagate in the new filter material. This biological filtration activity will be described in more detail later

Filtration

in this chapter. An additional benefit of this filter is that the pump can provide strong water circulation in the aquarium. These filters were "state of the art" at one time, and many people still use them exclusively. I have used one for over fifteen years and it is still running strong. However, it cannot compare with the mechanical and biological filtration efficiency of the wet/dry filters that will be discussed later. On the other hand, it does a good job and does not cost as much.

The external tank that uses the preformed inserts provides a major increase in convenience and ease of maintenance over the previously described filter. It also does a good job of filtration, but multiple units may be needed to filter larger tanks. The manufacturer will usually specify what size of tank the filter is designed to handle. Always stay on the conservative side of this number so that the filter is not operating at maximum capacity. Since most of these filters use the cascade method of water return, they provide the additional benefit of good surface disturbance.

External canister filters

Another popular mechanical filter is the external canister. This is a closed cylindrical shaped filter that contains a pump typically driven by an external motor through magnetic coupling. These filters usually sit in the bottom of the aquarium stand. The pump draws water from the aquarium and through the filter material, which is usually fiber floss, and then returns the water back to the aquarium. The overall efficiency of this type of filter is very similar to the external tanks described above. The main advantage of the canister is that it makes the aquarium look better by not having a big

Filtration

filter tank hanging off the back. As with the external tank filters described above, the canister filter also provides strong water circulation in the aquarium. However, they are not convenient to clean and require valves in the tubing that run between the filter and aquarium so that the canister can be isolated and removed. Figure 2 shows a typical external canister filter.

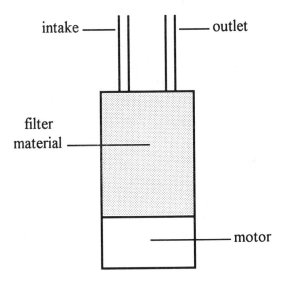

Figure 2. Typical external canister filter.

Corner bubbler filters

A popular filter for small freshwater tanks is the corner bubbler that uses air bubbles rising through a tube to draw water through filter floss and carbon. This type of filter is

Filtration

absolutely not suitable for a saltwater tank of any size. It provides neither adequate filtration nor good water circulation.

Protein skimmer

One of the best filtration systems you can use is the protein skimmer. This simple mechanism uses only fine air bubbles as the filter medium and does an excellent job of removing organic debris before it has a chance to be harmful.

Water is usually drawn into a protein skimmer by siphon action, and a separate pump returns it to the aquarium. The protein skimmer consists of a tall tube with an air bubbler of porous wood that produces extremely fine bubbles at the bottom. As water passes through the tube, air is pumped through the bubbler producing very fine bubbles that rise through the water. The air bubbles have a surface tension that causes them to adhere readily to any organic debris in the water. The organic debris rises to the top of the water with the bubbles and creates a foam. The foam is then collected in a container and routinely cleaned out. The large total surface area of the huge number of tiny bubbles with their good surface adhesion make this an extremely efficient filter mechanism.

For maximum efficiency, we want the bubbles to have plenty of time to adhere to any organic debris. One method used to increase the time the bubbles are in contact with the water, is to make the tube longer. This works fine, however, the tube can end up being so long that it is not practical. Another way of increasing the contact time is to slow down

Filtration

and control the flow of water through the skimmer. Water can be introduced into the bottom of the tube to rise with the bubbles and then run out of another tube in the side that takes it back to the pump. However, if we introduce the water at the top of the tube and make it flow against the direction of the air bubble stream, the contact time is greatly increased. This type of protein skimmer is called "counter current" and is the most efficient type.

Some aquarists are so impressed with the efficiency of the protein skimmer that they use it as the only filtration system on their aquariums. I am a strong advocate of the use of protein skimmers, and especially counter current protein skimmers, but believe that they should serve in combination with other filtration systems to provide maximum benefit. Manufacturers are also becoming convinced about the benefits of protein skimmers and have started combining them into some of their external tank filters. Figure 3 shows a typical counter current protein skimmer.

Diatomaceous earth filters
Another type of mechanical filter is a version of the external canister or tank that uses diatomaceous earth as a filter media rather than polyester fiber. Diatomaceous earth is an extremely fine filter media and does a very good job of cleaning the water. Many aquarists refer to the use of a diatomaceous earth filter as "polishing" the water. This type of filter is best used as part of the routine maintenance of an aquarium. During maintenance it can be run to help filter the organic debris and waste that gets stirred up. It is not recommended for full time operation.

Filtration

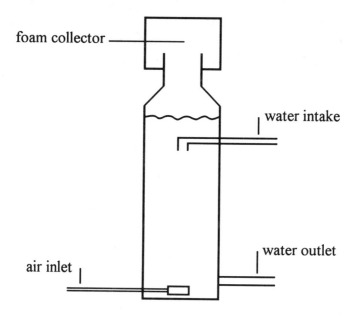

Figure 3. Typical counter current protein skimmer.

Molecular adsorption

A subset of mechanical filtration is chemical filtration, also known as molecular adsorption. The mechanism is the same as mechanical filtration, however the filter media is different and is used to absorb unwanted chemicals, rather than organic debris, from the water. Molecular absorption media can be used in conjunction with the filter floss or it can be placed by itself anywhere in the water flow. Activated carbon is by far the most widely used medium and is used to remove most unwanted gasses and chemicals. Activated carbon can be purchased loose and then placed in a

Filtration

mesh bag with a very tight weave so that the carbon does not fall out. Activated carbon can also be purchased in pre-bagged form. When purchasing activated carbon, be sure not to buy charcoal. Charcoal is also sold to remove chemicals however it has limited capacity to do so, and releases phosphates and other undesirable chemicals back into your aquarium. Other molecular adsorption media can be purchased in either mat form that you can cut to the size you need or as lose grains that can be placed in a bag just as described above for carbon. The most common of these other molecular absorption media are those that remove phosphate and nitrate.

Biological filtration

All of the major types of mechanical filters have been described above, so now we move on to the biological filters. The principal job of the biological filter is to break down the organic debris, such as the excretions of the fish and the compounds given of by decaying food, into less harmful substances.

To understand how a biological filter works, we need to discuss the makeup of organic waste. When organic matter decays, the nitrogen rich compound ammonia (NH_3) is created. Ammonia is also a primary waste product of fish and is released from the gills during respiration. Very little ammonia is excreted with the urine. Since ammonia is toxic to fish, it must be removed from the aquarium immediately and not allowed to build up. Fortunately, we are able to take advantage of knowledge developed by the sewage treatment industry so that we can effectively deal with ammonia and other nitrogen based toxic compounds. What we have learned

Filtration

is that ammonia can be reduced to nitrite (NO_2) when it comes in contact with specialized bacteria living on a substrate in the presence of water. These bacteria, called *Nitrosomonas*, consume ammonia as part of their metabolism and produce nitrite as a waste. Nitrite is also toxic; however, another specialized bacteria, called *Nitrobacter*, living in the same substrate will consume it and release nitrate (NO_3). Nitrate is still toxic to fish but at a greatly reduced level when compared to ammonia. The nitrate is kept under control by periodically changing part of the water in the aquarium. If partial water changes take place at a rate greater than nitrate is produced, it will never be allowed to build up to harmful levels. In the molecular absorption discussion above, nitrate absorption media was mentioned. This media helps control nitrate buildup but should only be used as an adjunct to control by partial water changes. A biological filter then is the one that allows the *Nitrosomonas* and *Nitrobacter* bacteria to live and consume ammonia and nitrite.

Nitrogen cycle

The entire process of establishing the bacteria for converting ammonia to nitrite and then to nitrate is called the "nitrogen cycle". This cycle takes place in all of our aquariums when we first set them up. The *Nitrosomonas* and *Nitrobacter* bacteria are present in the fish gut, and through excretions, will soon also be in the bottom and rock substrate of our aquariums and in the filters. The population of these bacteria will increase in the presence of the ammonia and nitrite that they consume. The nitrogen cycle can take weeks or months to finish in a new tank. This is because the level of ammonia must first increase in the aquarium, and then the

Filtration

population of the *Nitrosomonas* bacteria will follow. If we were to test our water daily we would see the level of ammonia rise to a peak and then drop off as the population of *Nitrosomonas* increased. The same series of events would be noted for nitrite and the *Nitrobacter* with the peak in the level of nitrite occurring after the peak in the level of ammonia. Figure 4 shows how the nitrogen cycle progresses in a new aquarium. The nitrogen cycle can be accelerated by the addition of these bacteria, which can be purchased at most aquarium shops. The nitrogen cycle will be discussed further in Chapter 12, Setting Up The Aquarium.

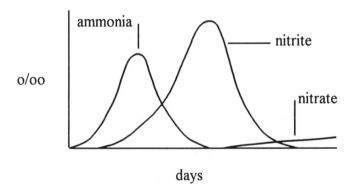

Figure 4. The nitrogen cycle.

Biological filtration in a mechanical filter

Earlier in this chapter we discussed how a mechanical filter can incorporate some biological filtration, and that it was beneficial to leave a small piece of the old floss in the filter when new floss was added. The old floss has existing colonies of *Nitrosomonas* and *Nitrobacter* bacteria and a piece of this floss can be used to "seed" the new filter. This helps

Filtration

to keep the biological filtration process going with a minimum of interruption. The biological filtration that is taking place in mechanical filters will never reach the levels possible in a true biological filter; however, we will gladly incorporate any extra filtration that we can.

Undergravel filters

Another type of biological filter designed for aquarium use is the undergravel filter. It consists of a series of inverted plastic trays placed under the bottom substrate. These inverted trays have perforations that allow the water to pass through them. Tubes are attached to these trays and these tubes extend upwards almost to the surface of the water. The tubes are either attached to a power head pump at the top or an air pump with an air stone at the bottom. Power heads are preferred because they provide a stronger water flow and avoid the misting problem caused by the air bubbles as described in Chapter 7, Water Circulation. Due to the pumping action of the power head or the suction induced by the rising bubbles, water is drawn downward through the substrate and then returned to the surface through the tubes. While the water is passing through the substrate and through the trays, organic waste is drawn down into the undergravel filter and processed by *Nitrosomonas* and *Nitrobacter* bacteria. Figure 5 shows a typical undergravel filter.

This system works well; however, eventually the substrate and the area under the inverted trays becomes loaded with sludge. After a year or so of operation, it often becomes necessary to remove this sludge. This means completely dismantling the tank, which is a major inconvenience to both

Filtration

you and the fish. These filters have an additional drawback. Should the power go off or if the power head fails, all of this sludge remains inside your tank where it can do the most harm. In spite of this, many aquarists have used undergravel filters successfully for years. These filters have an additional benefit of minimizing the number of pipes and tubes hanging off the back of your aquarium, thus making it much more attractive.

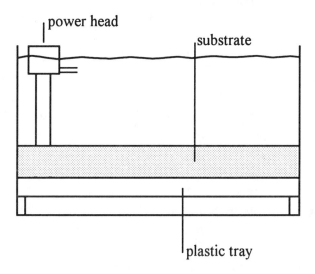

Figure 5. An undergravel filter.

Wet/dry or trickle filters

The next biological filter is the wet/dry or trickle filter. These filters do an exceptional job in the world of biological filtration. In order for complete and efficient biological filtration to take place we need very large surface areas for the *Nitrosomonas* and *Nitrobacters* to live on. Again taking a lesson from the sewage treatment industry, wet/dry filters use a substrate of round- or cube-shaped pieces made of plastic or ceramic. These substrate pieces are constructed with numerous small rod-like surfaces to provide a very large total surface area for the bacteria to colonize on. Another material used in wet/dry filters for the colonization of bacteria is a very long rectangular layer of floss on top of a matching plastic mesh. These two layers are rolled into a spiral and placed in the biological media chamber of the wet/dry filter. This material is referred to as double layer spiral or DLS.

So, now that we know about the biological filtration media, let's discuss how the wet/dry filter works. These filters are large and require space below or alongside your aquarium. They are typically made of acrylic, and outwardly they often look like another aquarium. Inside they have two main chambers. Water is siphoned from the aquarium into the first chamber, which is filled with the biological media (balls, cubes, or DLS). The water is evenly distributed over all of the media by either a rotating spray bar or by a drip plate that is full of holes. The spray bar mechanism and the drip plate each rest on ledges at the top of the biological medium and receive water from the siphon tube. The water falls over the filter medium and collects at the bottom of this chamber. The biological medium is not immersed in the water, rather it is subjected to a continuous trickle of water over it, thus the origination of the names "wet/dry" and "trickle," both of which are used to describe this type of filter. Since the biological substrate is not immersed in water, air helps with the chemical process. The bottom of the biological chamber connects to the second chamber which is actually a sump

Filtration

that collects all of the water and directs it through a hose to a pump that returns the water to the aquarium. Since this filter is large, it is possible to incorporate various mechanical and chemical filter media, as well as a protein skimmer, in the sump. This allows for a complete filtration system to be created. Figure 6 shows a typical wet/dry filter.

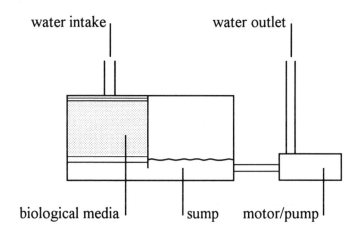

Figure 6. Typical wet/dry filter.

Skimming the surface water

A condition that exists in many saltwater aquariums is a film covering the surface of the water. This film is the result of various organic and inorganic debris that are captured by the surface tension of the water. It is beneficial if we can remove this film, and the best way to do this is by skimming the surface water into the filter system. This is done with a small box, called a skimmer box, with an open top and a series of slots cut into the top of the sides. This box

Filtration

is hung inside the aquarium and is connected to another box that hangs off the back of the aquarium by a siphon tube. The second box is called the overflow box. When the water flows down to the wet/dry filter from the overflow box, it is replaced by water siphoned from the skimmer box. The skimmer box is then filled by the surface water flowing through the slots. This is a very efficient way to skim the film off the surface water and is very common for wet/dry filters. This method is even used in some external tank filters. Figure 7 is a close up view of this type of surface skimmer arrangement.

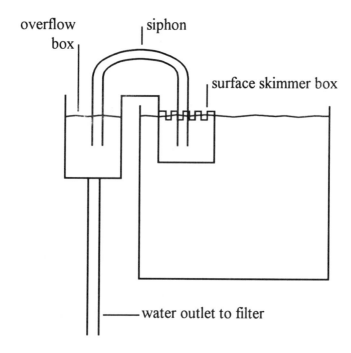

Figure 7. Surface skimmer for a wet/dry filter.

Filtration

Reverse siphon action

When the pump that returns water to the aquarium is turned off, water continues to be drawn into the wet/dry filter by siphon action from both the surface skimmer box and by reverse siphon action from the discharge tube of the pump. Once the water level drops lower than the slots on the skimmer box this part of the siphon action will stop. However, water will continue to be drawn through reverse siphon action into the pump discharge until the aquarium water level drops lower than the level of the pump discharge outlet inside the aquarium. If the pump discharge tube inside the aquarium is too low, the wet/dry filter will eventually overflow and you will have salt water all over the floor. So, some method of breaking this reverse siphon action must be incorporated. A very good method to use is to have the pump discharge tube outlet about an inch below the surface of the aquarium water. Immediately below, but not connected to the pump discharge tube, is a second tube. The second tube makes it possible to direct the return flow in any direction required. Since the discharge tube is very near the surface, there is no danger of overflowing the wet/dry filter when the pump is turned off. Figure 8 shows this arrangement.

All undergravel and wet/dry filters are sold with a manufacturer's recommendation of how large a tank they can handle. Once again be conservative so that your filter is not working at maximum capacity. For my 150-gallon mini-reef, I use a wet/dry filter designed to handle a 300-gallon tank together with a large protein skimmer and have been extremely pleased with the results.

Filtration

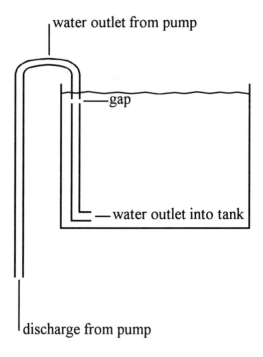

Figure 8. A pump discharge arrangement to prevent reverse siphon action.

Chapter 9

LIGHTS

As noted earlier, one of the natural conditions of a coral reef is lots of sunshine. Every day more is learned about the importance of sunlight and its effect on life both on land and in the ocean. The benefits of sunlight are not only biological but psychological as well. Many recent studies have shown that bright sunlight or even bright artificial lights have a profound effect on human behavior and can be used to treat various physical and psychological problems such as skin conditions and jet lag. Life on earth is guided by the diurnal cycle of light and darkness. The fish in the coral reef are no exception to this. So, to make conditions in our aquarium as close to natural as possible, we need to provide a diurnal cycle complete with bright lights that duplicate the sun's spectrum.

Photosynthesis
Beyond it's importance to fish, sunlight is of absolutely critical importance to many of the inhabitants of the reef. All algae require sunlight to perform photosynthesis, the process by which plants with chlorophyll use light, carbon dioxide, and water to create carbohydrates for consumption. This process also releases oxygen into the environment.

Algae and *zooxanthellae*
Most people think of algae as the slimy green moss that covers many stagnant bodies of water. While this is in-

Lights

deed algae, it is in an out of control situation due to excessive nutrients in the water. In a healthy coral reef the algae is in a natural balance with all other life forms and plays a vital role by consuming organic nutrients and by serving as a source of food for many other animals. Actually micro and macro algae grow on the reef and both can be quite beautiful. The need for strong sunlight is particularly important for animals such as the corals, giant clams, and anemones. These animals contain *zooxanthellae* which are algae cells that live in the tissues of the host in a symbiotic relationship. The *zooxanthellae* actually consume sunlight through photosynthesis and produce carbohydrates which provide much of the nutrition of the host animal. Without strong sunlight, the *zooxanthellae* die and then the animal itself dies. This is why silt and an excess of organic nutrients (debris) in the water are so harmful to a reef. The silt blocks out the sunlight and the excess nutrients cause the micro algae to grow out of control which can smother animals and further block out the light. When the light diminishes, the reef animals start to die. This creates more organic debris and pollution in the water leading to uncontrolled micro algae blooms. Unless brought under control quickly, the once pristine reef dies.

Absorption of light by water

Water absorbs light, and the deeper we dive the less bright our environment is. Different frequencies of light penetrate water to different depths. The red and yellow frequencies are absorbed within the first few tens of feet of water. Only the greens and blues penetrate deeper, with the blues penetrating deepest of all, sometimes beyond 100 feet if the water is clear enough. That is why everything looks bluish as

Lights

we dive deeper. However, if we take an artificial light with us and illuminate the fish, plants, and other animals on the bottom, we find that they are often quite colorful.

So, the lesson here is that sunlight is of great importance to fish and of life and death importance to the coral reef in general. What that means for our aquarium is this: if we are going to have just fish and perhaps a few invertebrates, we need to have a good source of light that approximates the spectrum of the sun and the diurnal cycle. If we are going to nurture a mini-reef, then we must provide even greater levels of light that duplicate the spectrum of sunlight and also have increased intensity in the frequencies that the *zooxanthellae* need to perform photosynthesis. Since this book is only concerned with the basics of keeping saltwater fish and not mini-reefs, our job is a little easier.

Light sources

There are two sources of light readily available to us: incandescent and fluorescent. Incandescent bulbs are compact, generate a lot of heat, and only partially duplicate the full spectrum of the sun. Because of this they are not recommended for aquarium use. The only exception to this are the new metal-halide bulbs that were designed specifically for reef use. They are very bright, provide a proper spectrum and generate lots of heat. Their use is recommended for serious mini-reef keeping.

By far the best light for most aquarium applications is fluorescent tubes. They can be purchased in different lengths to provide light over the entire length of the aquarium.

Lights

Fluorescent tubes do not consume much power and do not generate much heat. They also come in many different types that either duplicate natural sunlight or concentrate light in the frequencies that are most desirable for the *zooxanthellae*. For our fish tank, any of the fluorescent lights described as "daylight," "natural sunlight" or otherwise offered up as encouraging growth in plants are satisfactory.

How much light is necessary?

So, now we need to concern ourselves with how much light we really need for our fish. Using lights with reflectors, a nice bright tank can be created using a rule of thumb of 20 watts per square foot of water surface area. First determine the surface area of the top of your tank (length x width) in square feet, then multiply this number by 20 to determine how many watts you need. For example, if your tank is 48 inches by 12 inches, first convert inches to feet to get 4 feet by 1 foot and multiply to get a total of 4 square feet. Now multiply 4 by 20 to get 80 watts. This determination is for bulbs used with reflectors. If your lights do not have reflectors, then multiply your total number of watts by 2. This is because a bare tube radiates light in all directions and no more than one half will actually enter your aquarium and be of any use to your fish. Some bulbs come with a reflective material on one half of their inside surface. This material works just as well as an external reflector, and allows you to use less wattage than with bare tubes.

The number of 20 watts per square foot is a general guide and equates to an intensity of approximately 3600 lux per square foot. It is acceptable to use a higher intensity of

Lights

illumination. Most reef fish can stand very high levels of illumination; however, these levels are not really necessary unless you are keeping corals and macro algae in a mini-reef.

Many aquarium setups come with a hood and lights as part of the package. If not, you can purchase them separately. If you are really ambitious and understand electrical circuitry you can construct your own lights; however, I recommend that the new saltwater aquarist use standard packages and not experiment with constructing customized lights until more experience and understanding is gained.

As always, be careful when working around your lights. They will be operating at 110 volts just inches above the water. Make sure that they stay clean and dry and always remove any salt spray from them before it has a chance to dry and corrode the metal fittings. Always repair any lose or frayed wires immediately. Your life is too important to take chances when working around electricity.

Lights

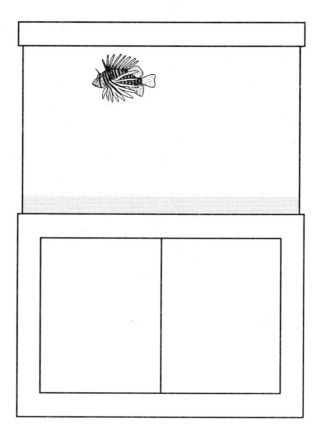

Chapter 10

TEMPERATURE

Maintaining a proper and constant temperature in your aquarium is vitally important to the health and survival of your fish. Coral reef fish are used to constant warm temperatures, and that is what we need to achieve in our aquariums. Typically, most reef fish are content with a temperature range of 72 to 82 degrees Fahrenheit. If you want to introduce fish from other water environments, pay attention to their temperature needs before you purchase them to make sure that they are compatible with the fish you already have.

To maintain a constant temperature, you may need either a heater or a chiller or perhaps both depending on the temperature required and the ambient temperature of the room and the seasonal weather temperatures. Most aquariums will require water temperatures which are approximately the same as the temperature in air-conditioned rooms. Since the evaporation of water has a cooling effect, most aquariums will require only a heater to maintain a proper temperature. However, if you live in a very warm environment without air conditioning or if you choose fish that require colder temperatures you, may also need a chiller.

Heaters

Heaters are small, self-contained, inexpensive, and easy to use. They consist of a heating coil placed in a glass

Temperature

tube that is immersed in the water. The top of the tube is closed off and contains an adjustable thermostat that controls when the heater turns on and off. When the heater turns on, the temperature of water in the immediate vicinity increases. As water circulation takes place in the aquarium, an even temperature is maintained.

If the heater is too small, it will operate continuously, which shortens its life, and it will never keep the aquarium warm enough. So, it is important to purchase a heater of the proper size. Heaters are identified according to how many watts they provide and what size of tank in gallons they are suited for. The general recommendation is that you need two to five watts per gallon. For example, a 50-gallon tank would require a heater between 100 and 250 watts. If possible, pick a heater at the top end of this range. This will ensure that you have plenty of heating capacity available and the heater will not have to work as hard and will last longer. Also, you do not want a heater that is so long that it touches the bottom of your tank. Heaters can be installed by clamping them to the top of the tank or by attaching them to the back glass with suction cups. These attachments are included with the heater and can also be purchased separately. Some heaters are waterproof and designed to be totally submerged and held in place with suction cups. Before you place any heater completely under water, be sure that it is designed to be submerged and is in good condition!

Chillers

If your tank is too warm, you should first explore some techniques to bring the temperature down before you

Temperature

decide to purchase a chiller. Since water cools as it evaporates, you should encourage this evaporation. Make sure that lots of ambient air passes across the surface of your water. If the top of your tank has removable glass panels remove them to help this evaporation. Some lights can generate enough heat to warm up the water. If this is the case in your aquarium, raise the lights an inch or more to let additional air pass underneath. If the top of your aquarium is enclosed by a canopy, it may even be necessary to use a fan to provide sufficient air flow across the top of the water and help remove the heat from your lights. If your filter system is totally enclosed in the bottom of your stand, check to make sure that this area is not storing heat from the filter pump motor. If so, this heat can add additional temperature to the water as it passes through the filter. If this is the case be sure to provide additional ventilation to this area of the stand. Also observe the location of your aquarium to see if it is being heated by direct sunshine or perhaps warm air coming from a refrigerator, oven or other appliance. It may be necessary to move your aquarium to a cooler room. It is also possible to lower the temperature by placing jugs of frozen water in the sump of the wet/dry filter. Fill a clean, used, plastic milk jug three quarters full of water and freeze it. Put the cap on the jug and then place it in the sump. As the water in the jug melts, replace it with another frozen jug as necessary, but be careful to not lower the temperature too quickly.

If your aquarium requires a chiller, be prepared to spend several hundred dollars and have some extra space available for the unit. Early chillers consisted of modified cooling systems from refrigerators and were large and awk-

Temperature

ward. It is now possible to purchase chillers designed specifically for aquariums. They are smaller than the early models, but they still require a fair amount of space. Typically, only very serious aquarists will take on the challenge of using a chiller.

If you absolutely must have a chiller, you will need a convenient area such as the bottom cabinet of your stand for the chiller to sit. Chillers are sold according to how many gallons have to be cooled and how many degrees of temperature need to be removed. This information is used to determine what size motor and compressor is required to do the job. You will probably have to special order the chiller from an aquarium shop.

Chapter 11

OTHER EQUIPMENT

The marketplace is full of other pieces of equipment for your aquarium. However, you probably do not need much, if any, of it. The following is a brief description of the more common equipments that you will encounter.

Wave and surge makers

Wave makers create waves by dumping water into the tank at regular intervals. Surge makers periodically turn pumps or power heads on and off so that a back and forth surge is set up in the tank. These devices are great for circulation; however, they are not really required for the fish aquarium. They are normally only used on mini-reefs by very serious aquarists.

Ultraviolet sterilizers

Ultraviolet (UV) sterilizers are useful for killing bacteria, viruses, and fungi that are freely swimming in your water. These devices consist of an ultraviolet lamp housed in a container that allows water to pass over the surface of the lamp. Typically a UV sterilizer is placed in line with the return flow of water from the pump to the tank. The effectiveness of these lamps depends on the intensity of the ultraviolet light and the length of time that the water is in contact with the surface of the lamp.

Other Equipment

Most aquarists do not bother with a UV sterilizer and get along fine without them. Others only use them on a part time basis as adjunct to the routine maintenance. Some use them full time and believe strongly in the benefits they provide.

Two precautions need to be observed if you choose to purchase one of these lamps. First, the ultraviolet lamp produces lots of heat and should never be turned on without water flowing through it. This will prevent overheating and a possible fire hazard. Second, never look directly at the ultraviolet lamp when it is turned on. In operation, these lamps are fully enclosed and only have a small indicator light to let you know that they are turned on. If you disassemble your lamp or turn it on with one of the plumbing fittings removed (which you should never do), do not look at the lamp. If you do look at it, severe eye damage or even blindness is possible.

Ozonizers
In a constant effort to remove organic debris, some aquarists have turned to ozonizers. Ozone (O_3) is an ionized form of oxygen and has an even greater oxidizing potential. The benefit of ozone is that it increases the oxidization of organic debris and it can even kill bacteria. The use of ozone must be precisely regulated because too much ozone can be harmful or even fatal to your fish. Recent designs and developments have resulted in ozonizers that are safe and convenient to use. However, most ozonizers are used by serious aquarists with their mini-reefs.

Chapter 12

SETTING UP THE AQUARIUM

We have covered the basics of saltwater aquariums and the equipment that supports them. So it is time to start putting everything together. Based on personal desire, money available, and room, decide what size and kind of tank and stand you want and purchase them.

Give everything a good cleaning before you put them in place because once they are set up and the tank is full of water, cleaning is much harder to do. Also, give your stand a final inspection to make sure that it is properly assembled and that all joints are secure. When cleaning the inside of the tank do not use soap or cleansers of any kind. If there is dirt or scum to be removed use water, some salt and a cloth or soft woven plastic pad. This combination will remove almost any debris you find in the tank. Anything else in a glass tank can be removed with a single edged razor blade used very carefully. When cleaning the glass do not use an abrasive pad as this may cause scratches. If you have an acrylic tank be especially careful and only use soft cloth to avoid scratches.

Setting the tank and stand in place

As mentioned in Chapter 4, Stands, you may need to add additional support to the floor that your aquarium will be sitting on. If extra support is required, put it in place before

Setting Up The Aquarium

you add water to the tank. As you set up the stand and tank, make sure that you have enough room between the tank and the wall for all of the external filter tanks, tubes, etc. that you will be using. Also make sure that you have an electrical outlet located conveniently nearby. Pay attention to how sunlight enters the room throughout the day, so that you can avoid placing the aquarium in direct sunlight. Finally, perform an initial check to make sure that the top of the tank is level along both the length and width. If the top of the tank is not level, place flat wood or metal shims under the stand as necessary.

Undergravel filter substrate

If you are going to use an undergravel filter, now is the time to put in into position. Cover the filter with 2-3 inches of sand that is approximately 1/8 to 1/4 of an inch in diameter or follow the manufacture's recommendations. Next, add the riser tubes and power heads. Finally, add whatever rocks or decorations that you want.

Substrate

If you will not be using an undergravel filter, now is the time to add 1/2 inch or less of your bottom substrate material and whatever rock decorations that you want to use. If you do not have them now, they can be added later, but that is a bit more of a mess.

Adding water

Before you start adding water it is a good idea to check it for ammonia, nitrite and nitrate. Details on testing water can be found in Chapter 14, Maintaining The Aquarium.

Setting Up The Aquarium

Normally the fresh water will be good, but occasionally not. If your water is questionable, try to find a good source of water or run your water through a carbon filter before adding it to your tank. A carbon filter is made by taking a piece of PVC tubing two inches wide and three feet long and adding a reducer with a hose fitting on each end. Before capping both ends, fill the tube with activated carbon. Then pass all of your water through this filter before adding it to your aquarium.

Now you can start adding the water and salt. It is a good idea to pre-dissolve the salt in a bucket of warm water so that you have a highly concentrated saltwater mix. Add this mix to the fresh water during the filling process and you will be able to get an accurate salinity measurement quicker. If you have access to a garden hose, the filling process is greatly simplified. If not, then you need to carry water in buckets, jugs, or whatever else you have available. As you add the water, continue to pay attention to the level the water will take relative to the top surfaces of the aquarium. You want to make sure that when the aquarium is full, the water is the same distance from the top of the tank all the way around. If not, stop and add thin boards or metal shims under the stand to level everything out.

Heater

Put your heater in place and let it adjust to the ambient water temperature for 30 minutes before plugging it in. This will keep it from experiencing thermal shock and breaking the glass tube when it is turned on.

Setting Up The Aquarium

External tank filter

If you are using an external tank filter, install the filter media and other parts and put the unit in place. Since these are normally self contained units, they require very little plumbing or extra connections.

If you need to establish a siphon between the aquarium and the external tank, you can use this easy method. Add water to the filter tank so that the bottom of the siphon tube is covered. Then insert a section of air line tubing into the siphon until the end of the tubing is at the top of the inside of the siphon. Now, with both ends of the siphon covered with water, suck the air out through the air line tube. As you remove the air from the siphon tube, the water level inside it will begin to rise. Continue until the siphon tube is full and water starts passing through it. This will bring the water in the aquarium and the filter tank to the same level.

External canister filter

If you are using a canister filter, the set up is slightly more complicated because you need to run hoses or tubing from the filter to the aquarium and back. Connect one tube from the canister discharge to the water discharge pipe in the aquarium. Connect the other tube from the inlet pipe in the aquarium to the canister inlet. Finally, place filter floss or any other filter media to be used inside the canister following the manufacture's recommendations.

Wet/dry filter

If you are using a wet/dry filter you have even more work to do. First, install all of the necessary tubing and plumb-

Setting Up The Aquarium

ing from the aquarium to the biological chamber and from the sump to the pump. Next, complete the circuit from the pump back to the aquarium. Since lots of tubes and hoses are involved here, take your time and work carefully to avoid the inconvenience of leaks when you start the system. Next, fill the biological chamber with either the ball- or cube-shaped filter media, or the double-layer spiral. Often the overflow box and the tray in the top of the biological box will have a provision for foam filter blocks, floss mats or even lose filter floss. Now is the time to put them in place. Also, add any other filter media that you will use. For example, the area where the biological chamber opens to the sump is often designed so that you can add foam blocks for extra filtration, or perhaps bags of activated carbon or other media.

Protein skimmer

The sump of your wet/dry filter is a great place for a protein skimmer, so, if you are going to use one, set it up here if at all possible. If your protein skimmer will not fit in the sump or if you are using a protein skimmer in conjunction with an external tank or canister filter, you will have some extra plumbing connections to make.

Electrical connections

If you are going to use a power head or auxiliary pump in your aquarium, now is the time to add it. Next, set your lights in place. At this point you probably have several things that need to be connected to the electrical outlet. If you have more plugs than outlets, use a power strip rather than extension cords. Power strips will safely accommodate the extra plugs and have the added safety of an overload circuit breaker.

Setting Up The Aquarium

It is very important to arrange your electrical wires in an orderly manner, so that you can easily determine which wire serves which function. This avoids confusion and possible unsafe conditions. Also, give each of your wires a drip loop before they are plugged into the receptacle or power strip. Create the drip loop by allowing some of the electrical cord to hang lower than the outlet that it is plugged into. It is always possible for salt water to be splashed or otherwise find its way to an electrical cord. When this happens the water will run down the cord and possibly into the receptacle causing electrical shorts, corrosion, and generally unsafe conditions. The drip loop will allow the water to drip off the cord at its lowest point before it goes into the receptacle. This is much safer and gives you the opportunity to routinely inspect the cords for evidence of water so that you can fix whatever is causing this problem.

Starting the filter pump

Once all of the pieces are in place and filled with water, turn on the filter pump. It may take a few seconds for the pump to start moving water and in the meantime you may see lots of bubbles being introduced into the aquarium. This is normal and nothing to worry about unless the bubbles continue and the pump does not pump water. If this is the case, check for leaks and make sure that there is an adequate supply of water available to the pump so that it is not running dry.

Once everything is running and the water is circulating, you are well on your way. Your water will probably be a little cloudy. This is normal, and is caused by undissolved

Setting Up The Aquarium

salt particles and any remaining dust from the aquarium substrate. The salt will eventually completely dissolve and the filters will remove the dust.

Let the aquarium run for several days. During this time the water will reach the proper temperature, and you can adjust the salinity as necessary. This gives you the opportunity to ensure that everything is operating correctly, and you can make whatever small adjustment are necessary. It also allows time for any chlorine to escape from the water (if you are on city water). Take advantage of this time to test your water for pH, ammonia, nitrite, and nitrate and record your findings in a notebook with the date. If any of these conditions are out of the desired ranges, either add chemical treatments or replace the water as necessary. Normally all measurements will be good.

Adding fish

Now we have arrived at the point where you can start adding fish. It is important to go slow at this point because the nitrogen cycle has not started and your filters will not be able to handle many fish. If you add too many fish too fast, the excretions will overwhelm your filter, a buildup of ammonia will occur, and your fish will suffer and may even die. The proper way to start is to pick two or three of the heartiest, least aggressive, and least expensive fish that you will be keeping and add them to the tank at this time. You want to use hearty fish so that they have the greatest chance of surviving the start-up phase of your tank. You also want to add the least aggressive fish first so that they can establish their own territory. If you start with aggressive fish first and then

Setting Up The Aquarium

add the more timid fish later, the aggressive fish will harass, nip at, and maybe even kill the less aggressive fish, all in the name of territorial dominance. Finally, if something unfortunate goes wrong and the fish die, it is better for your finances if the fish did not cost a lot of money.

At this point we need to discuss the proper way to add fish to your aquarium. You will bring these fish home in plastic bags about half-full of water. Many people get worried about the fish having enough oxygen while being transported in the bags. While this is of concern, you only need to worry about it if your fish will be in the bags for more than three to four hours. It is more important to keep the water in the bag at a constant temperature. The best way to do this is to place the bags in an ice chest (without any ice) and take them home as soon as possible. Do not be tempted to run several errands after you have purchased your fish because you risk causing the temperature of the water in the bags to raise or lower significantly. This will cause the fish to become severely stressed or even die. Once the fish are home place the bags into the aquarium water for 30 minutes so that, the temperatures even out. When you are ready to release the fish, open the bag and pour the fish and water into a net and catch the water in a bucket. We do not want to add any foreign water into our tank, and catching the fish in a net and discarding the water takes care of that for us. Then, release the fish into the aquarium. Always use a big net so that the fish does not suffer any physical damage. To be sure that you are adding a healthy fish to your aquarium, you may want to first place it in a quarantine aquarium for a few days. This allows you to observe it closely for any signs of illness or

Setting Up The Aquarium

parasites before you introduce it into your display aquarium. If you detect any problems with the fish, either take it back to the shop or treat it. Chapter 17, Marine Fish Diseases, describes the more common illness and how to treat them.

As the fish excrete their waste and as food you give them goes uneaten, ammonia will start to build up. Since the *Nitrosomonas* and *Nitrobacter* already exist in the fish, they will become present in the aquarium and start to multiply and colonize the various substrates in the tank and the filters. Over a period of weeks, their population increases until there is a sufficient number to consume the ammonia and nitrites that are present in the tank. During this process the level of ammonia will rise to a peak and then drop, hopefully to a level of zero parts per thousand. The same thing will happen with the nitrites; however, this curve will lag a little behind the ammonia curve. It is important that you test your water several times a week during this period so that you can monitor the progress of the nitrogen cycle. After the cycle is completed, you can safely add more fish, but add them slowly. Even though the nitrogen cycle is completed, it still takes a few days for the *Nitrosomonas* and *Nitrobacter* to multiply to accommodate the increased ammonia and nitrite loads presented by more fish.

How many fish can be kept

One question that always comes up is "how many fish can be kept in an aquarium?". The precise answer depends on how big your aquarium is and what kind of filtration you have. For example, a wet/dry filter with a protein skimmer will support quite a few more fish than an external

Setting Up The Aquarium

tank filter on the same size aquarium. For an aquarium with external tank, canister, or an undergravel filter, my rule of thumb is to keep one inch of fish for each two and a half gallons of water. By this rule, a 50-gallon aquarium could hold a maximum of 20 one inch fish, or perhaps two fish five inches long and five fish two inches long. If you have a wet/dry filter and protein skimmer you may be able to keep a few more fish. Each experienced aquarist will have their own rule of thumb and not all of them agree with me or each other. I can only recommend what works best for me. Above all else, pay strict attention to your fish and if they start showing any signs of stress or illness, do not add any more until you are satisfied that you know what caused the condition, and that it has been corrected.

Chapter 15, Marine Fish, describes the more common reef fish that are suitable for an aquarium to help you make your decisions on which ones to keep. Chapter 16, Invertebrates, provides an overview of invertebrates that are suitable for your aquarium. Chapter 18, Introduction To Mini-Reefs, provides an introduction to this specialized type of aquarium. Keeping corals and macro algae in a mini reef requires special equipment, techniques, and knowledge and should not be attempted until you have mastered keeping fish only aquariums.

Chapter 13

FEEDING THE FISH

When it comes to feeding our fish, the goal once again is to duplicate natural foods as much as possible. However, this is often hard to do. Tangs for example require lots of algae in their diet and many aquariums may not have enough for them. In cases like this, we use other foods to provide the fish with their essential nutrients while trying to keep the food we give the fish as close to natural as possible.

The first step is to learn what foods your fish require for good health and growth. To help with this, Chapter 15, Marine Fish, provides information on the foods that various common aquarium fish prefer. It is also useful to ask the people at the aquarium shop where you purchased your fish what they were feeding your fish and how well it was eating. If the fish requires a highly specialized diet, you may want to wait until you have more experience with your aquarium and fish before you take on this additional responsibility. If we are going to bring fish home with us, we need to be sure that we can provide the proper conditions, food, and care that they require.

Any good salt water aquarium shop will have a large selection of live, frozen, and prepared foods available for our fish. Additionally, we can provide many desirable foods directly from our kitchens. In general, all fish prefer living

Feeding The Fish

foods to frozen or processed foods. So, we will start our discussions with live foods.

Live foods

It is important that we be very careful about what we put into our aquariums, and this includes the food we feed our fish. Sometimes, live food brings with it unwanted bacteria or debris. When you start preparing a portion of live food, always drain off all of the original water. Then, put the food in a container of fresh water for several minutes. This will often kill the various salt water bacteria and provide a bath to remove any debris. The easiest way to do this is to pour the live food into a fine mesh net to let the salt water drain off. Then, hold the net under a stream of running fresh water for a minute and place the living food in a container of fresh water. Let this stand for a few minutes. Next, pour the food back into your net, give it a final rinse and release the food into your tank.

Live brine shrimp

A staple of marine fish diet is living brine shrimp (*Artemia salina*). Most aquarium shops sell live brine shrimp in bags or containers of water. It is best to store your live brine shrimp in a small tank with an air bubbler to keep the water in motion. However, they can be stored for a few days in a cool spot such as a basement or perhaps in a warmer section of your refrigerator. Brine shrimp live in salt lakes and other areas that have a greater salinity than the open ocean. Since these areas are often subject to radical changes in the height of the water table, brine shrimp have developed eggs with a hard protein shell that allows the outside of the egg to

Feeding The Fish

dry out and endure long periods of dryness. When the egg is again submerged in salt water, it will hatch. This capability makes it possible for the aquarium shops to sell dried brine shrimp eggs for us to hatch at home in our own hatcheries.

There are several ways to hatch brine shrimp from eggs. One of the easiest methods is to buy a hatchery and eggs at your aquarium shop. However, if you want to make your own hatchery, you can use the following technique. You will need a glass jug or other glass container that holds approximately one gallon of water. Fill the container with water and salt mix to achieve a salinity of around 35 o/oo and keep the temperature at about 75 degrees Fahrenheit. Add the eggs and use an air pump and stone to keep the water circulating. Under these conditions the brine shrimp should hatch in a day or two. The newly hatched brine shrimp can be fed to your fish immediately; however, you need to avoid including any of the protein shells. These shells are very hard to digest and can cause constipation and distress in your fish. To separate the shells, first remove the air stone from the container allowing the brine shrimp to swim around and the more dense shells to sink to the bottom. Now you can safely siphon off the brine shrimp. If you prefer, you can siphon off the shells and discard them. Your fish will also love full grown brine shrimp, and you can easily raise them to this size in the hatchery if it is big enough. To do this, add a very small amount of yeast to serve as food for the growing brine shrimp. As an alternative, you can move the young brine shrimp into a small aquarium that has a good light source (even daylight is good). The light will stimulate algae growth to provide a natural food source for the brine shrimp. Finally,

Feeding The Fish

provide good circulation with an air pump and air stone.

Live bloodworms

Another good live food is the larvae of the midge fly (*Chironomidae*). Because the larvae are red and shaped like a very skinny worm they have the common name of bloodworm. While the name and the description may seem unsavory, be assured that fish love them and they are really not any more of a bother to prepare than brine shrimp. However, raising bloodworms is much more difficult, so you are better off buying these from your aquarium shop.

Live whiteworms

Yet another good live food is the whiteworm (*Enchytraeid*). Whiteworms are a little over an inch long and live in compost heaps and other such areas. Again, it is best to purchase these from the aquarium shop.

Live *Tubifex* worms

Another live food that you will hear about is *Tubifex* worms. These worms are found in sewage ponds, drainage ditches, and stagnant water. As a result, they typically are loaded with bacteria and other pollutants. These worms have been used by aquarists in the past, which is why you will hear of them today. Avoid feeding live *Tubifex* worms because they can easily cause illness and possibly even kill your fish.

Frozen brine shrimp

Among the most popular of frozen foods is brine shrimp. These are fed by cutting off a portion and thawing it

Feeding The Fish

out in fresh water. Then, drain off any cloudiness and give the rest to the fish. Frozen brine shrimp avoids much of the hassle of feeding live brine shrimp, but the fish lose a little because the food is not fresh and has lost some of its nutritional value. While fish can be raised on frozen brine shrimp, they are healthier if you also give them a variety of other foods. Frozen brine shrimp, as well as many other foods, can be cut into portions suitable for feeding and saved in a sealable container in your freezer.

Other frozen foods

Besides brine shrimp, you will find a wide variety of other frozen foods at your aquarium shop. These include such items as chopped shrimp, clams, krill, and squid. Also, you may find frozen vegetation such as kelp. All of these are good and provide important variety for your fish.

Flake food

You can also buy many different kinds of dry flaked foods. These are good for your fish, and are often enriched with vitamins, but should only be used as a supplement to your regular foods.

Foods prepared in the kitchen

Another good source of food is your kitchen. Many aquarists place small leaves of lettuce in their aquariums for the fish to feed on. This is especially good for fish that normally need eat lots of algae. Other vegetables such as small heads of broccoli or lettuce can be used. It is necessary to blanche the vegetables momentarily in boiling water to break down the cellulose to help the fish digest these foods. You

Feeding The Fish

can make or buy little clips that hold the vegetables in place so they do not get drawn into the filter. Fresh fish filets, squid, clams, oysters, and crab meat can also be fed. These meats can be cut into either small or large chunks to appeal to a variety of fish. Larger fish, such as the lionfish, will benefit from these chopped meats.

How much and how often

When you feed your fish, do not give them more than they can eat in five minutes. Any more than this and you can end up with excess food floating to the bottom of the aquarium or drawn into the filter. This uneaten food unnecessarily increases the biological load on your filter and can cause problems in your aquarium. In the literature you will find many recommendations on how often to feed your fish ranging from daily to once a week. I have had good success feeding my fish every other day and recommend this for you to start. Watch your fish carefully to see if they are taking the food readily and if their color is good. Also, note if they have plenty of energy and generally look healthy and happy. Depending on your impressions of how the fish are doing, you can then experiment with other schedules. Do not worry if you miss a feeding. The fish will still be able to pick at algae growth and many other things they find in the aquarium. They can go for a week between feedings, but this puts them under stress and jeopardizes their nutrition and health and should not be done except in an emergency.

Chapter 14

MAINTAINING THE AQUARIUM

Now that your aquarium is up and running and you are slowing adding fish, you need to start a program of routine maintenance. The best practice is to perform maintenance routinely once per week. Get into the habit of doing this and your aquarium will remain pristine and your fish will be happy and healthy. This maintenance will keep your aquarium a beautiful showcase, a real living jewel.

Inspect the aquarium and equipment
On maintenance day, start by conducting a thorough safety and operational inspection of all mechanical and electrical devices. Look for leaks, dripping water, lose connections, frayed wires, and anything else that could be a potential problem. Repair anything that needs attention. Next, thoroughly examine the inside of your tank for any dead fish and remove them immediately. Also, check out all of the other fish for signs of sickness. Common fish diseases and their cures will be discussed in Chapter 17, Marine Fish Diseases.

Check the water quality
Continue your maintenance by checking the quality of the water. Start this process by smelling the water at the top of your tank. It should smell clean and healthy like an ocean. If you detect the scent of onions, ammonia, or anything else, your aquarium needs serious attention. Then, move

Maintaining The Aquarium

on to actual testing of the pH, ammonia, nitrite, and nitrate. Various test kits are available that use a variety of test methods such as dissolving dry tables in a sample of the water or adding chemicals one drop at a time to the sample and noting color changes. For a healthy tank, you want a pH of 8.3 and zero parts per million (ppm) of ammonia, nitrite, and nitrate. If the pH is off, it can be adjusted with chemical additives. If the ammonia and nitrite levels are a little above zero ppm or if the nitrate is above 10 ppm, your aquarium is in need of a good cleaning and partial water change. If the levels are significantly elevated, your aquarium needs an immediate serious cleaning and a major water change. Table 4 describes the ranges of acceptable and unhealthy levels of ammonia, nitrite, and nitrate.

	parts per million		
	ideal	borderline	dangerous
Ammonia NH_3	0	.1 - .5	above .5
Nitrite NO_2	0	.1 - .5	above .5
Nitrate NO_3	0 - 10	10 - 40	above 40

Table 4. Acceptable and unhealthy ranges of ammonia, nitrite and nitrate in a marine aquarium.

Many other kits are available to test for such things as copper, phosphate, calcium, and alkalinity. While any attempt to improve water quality is desirable, it is not normally necessary to test beyond pH, ammonia, nitrite, and nitrate. As you gain experience and knowledge, you may want to test your water more thoroughly.

Maintaining The Aquarium

When you have finished testing the water, be sure to record the results in a log book along with the date. As time passes, the information in the log book will be very useful and will help you increase your knowledge and improve your aquarium keeping techniques.

Cleaning the tank

Now it is time to start the actual cleaning. Use a cloth, a soft plastic scrubber, or some other suitable device to remove the algae buildup on the inside of the aquarium glass. Be careful to use soft materials to avoid scratching the glass or acrylic. The plastic blade of an automobile window ice scraper works well for glass tanks, but should not be used on acrylics.

Some aquarists suggest that you not clean the back wall of the aquarium and let the algae build up for a natural effect. This is fine if you have your algae under control, and it is not growing wildly all over your tank. Otherwise, the back of your tank will start to look rather messy. If you do not have much algae growing in your tank, you may want to skip cleaning the back side so that your algae eating fish have some extra to graze on. Personally, if my aquarium has a good healthy growth of algae on the rocks, I go ahead and clean the back side.

Next, using an old tooth brush and a turkey baster, remove any excess algae growth and debris from the rocks. We want a healthy, but not an abundant, growth of algae in our aquariums. By routinely cleaning the rocks and inside walls, we help keep the algae growth under control.

Maintaining The Aquarium

A benefit of algae is that it consumes organic debris in the aquarium. By removing the algae you are actually "harvesting" part of the organic load and making your aquarium a safer place for your fish to live. However, as you clean the sides you will notice that you are releasing lots of algae and scum back into the water along with all of the consumed organic waste. It is very important to filter this new organic waste out of your aquarium water. This can be done two ways. One way is to continue to run your filter until all of the debris is removed and then give it a good cleaning. Another way is to shut off your filter while you are cleaning your aquarium and use an auxiliary filter for an hour or two to clean up this debris. This will reduce the organic load that your primary filter has to deal with when you turn it back on.

Cleaning the substrate

To remove the detritus and organic debris that has fallen to the bottom of the tank, use a large siphon tube to "vacuum" the substrate. Figure 9 shows a typical siphon tube that is used for this purpose. To use this siphon tube, you will need a large container to catch the water that is siphoned out. A very good container to use is one of the white five gallon buckets with a handle, such as those that paint and other construction materials come in. These buckets can be purchased at most hardware stores. Actually, any good, sturdy container will work fine; however, I prefer the bucket because of the handle. Put the siphon tube in the water and place the other end in the bucket. When you are ready, start the siphon by sucking on the end of the tube. Guide the siphon tube along the bottom of the tank until all of the sub-

Maintaining The Aquarium

strate has been cleaned. The large end of the siphon tube will pick up the bottom substrate but not let it be siphoned into the container. The siphoned off water will be full of organic debris and will be very cloudy and murky. Take a good look at it and consider how much better off your fish are now that it is removed from their environment. Next, remove the large siphon tube from the rubber hose and use the end of the hose to siphon up the detritus and waste that has accumulated beneath and between the rocks. Look around the aquarium for anything that was missed and clean it up with the siphon. All of the water that has been siphoned off now needs to be replaced with a fresh mix of salt water.

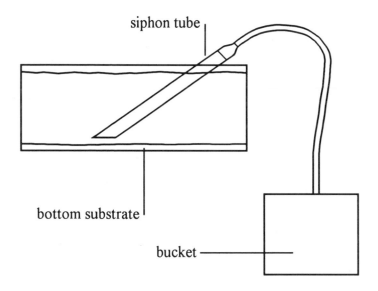

Figure 9. Siphon tube for cleaning the bottom substrate.

Maintaining The Aquarium

Partial water changes

While siphoning detritus and organic debris out of the aquarium you are performing another valuable task. That is the partial replacement of the aquarium water. As discussed in Chapter 8, Filtration, biological filtration converts the ammonia to nitrite and then into nitrate. Although nitrate can exist at higher concentrations in the aquarium than ammonia or nitrite, we really want it to be as low as possible and zero ppm is the goal. By routinely siphoning off part of the water and replacing it with new salt water, you are removing some of the nitrate and diluting the rest. You should remove and replace about 15-20 percent of your aquarium water each month. You can adjust how much water you siphon off during your routine maintenance so that you achieve this amount each month. Replacing part of the salt water routinely also helps replace trace elements that the fish consume directly from the salt water. So, routinely siphoning off accumulated detritus and organic waste and the water that comes with it goes a very long way toward keeping your aquarium healthy.

The replacement water should be prepared in advance in clean gallon jugs or other suitable containers. The goal is for the replacement water to be as close to the aquarium water in salinity and temperature as possible. This causes less stress on the fish as the new water is added.

Maintaining the filters

Next, remove and replace any filter floss, pads or foam blocks. If necessary, remove the external tank or canister filters as well as the siphon and discharge tubes and clean

Maintaining The Aquarium

them also. The tubes are best cleaned with bottle brushes and tooth brushes. Since the wet/dry filters depend on biological filtration, do not take these filters apart for cleaning. It is good enough to just replace the floss or foam and clean the various overflow boxes and siphon tubes that provide water to these filters.

Keep a record of when you last replaced your chemical filters such as activated carbon and replace them if necessary. Generally, you can leave these filters in place for three months. However, routinely inspect them to see if they are getting covered with debris and renew them if necessary even if three months have not passed. Also, note if the water is less than crystal clear. If so, then the carbon filter absolutely has to be changed so that it can help clean up these impurities.

Final cleaning
You may have dripped some water across the outside of your aquarium and stand during the cleaning so now clean all of these items. Wipe the excess salt water off the outside of the tank and stand with a soft cloth and fresh water and dry with a soft towel. The outside of the tank can then be cleaned with a common glass cleaner. If your stand is made of wood you should periodically treat it with lemon oil or a similar product to protect it from the effects of salt water. Also clean up any spilled water and salt crust from the lights and anywhere else you find it.

Between cleanings
You should inspect your aquarium every day to make

Maintaining The Aquarium

sure that all the inhabitants are alive and healthy and the electrical and mechanical devices are working properly. Take what ever action is required to correct any problems you discover.

Evaporation

As time passes, water will evaporate from the aquarium causing the overall water level to drop. Evaporation removes the water but leaves the salt behind. So, you have a constant amount of salt dissolved in a smaller quantity of water leading to an increased concentration and thus a higher salinity. The only thing that needs to be done is to simply add fresh (no salt mix) water to the aquarium to replace the amount that has evaporated. The amount that evaporates depends on the ambient temperature, humidity, and the surface area of your aquarium. My 150-gallon mini-reef needs about one gallon of water a day to compensate for evaporation.

Algae blooms

One of the most common problems that an aquarist will face is uncontroled algae blooms. When this happens the various substrates become covered with green hair-like algae and the water can even have a greenish tint. The first step in controlling an algae bloom is to recognize that algae requires light and organic nutrients (debris) to grow. Obviously if algae requires light to grow and we removed all sources of light the algae would die off. Unfortunately, this would also have a harmful effect on our other marine creatures. So, the trick is to cut back on the number of hours per day the lights are on and perhaps even cut back on the inten-

Maintaining The Aquarium

sity. The amount to cut back needs to be determined by experimenting. Since sunlight also stimulates algae growth be sure to check to see if the sun is shining on your aquarium. If so, you may have to use sun shades or curtains on the windows to block the light or maybe even move the aquarium.

The other condition that algae thrives on is excess organic debris (nutrients). An algae bloom is often a strong indication that the organic load in your aquarium is greater than your filters can handle. The cure here is to thoroughly clean the aquarium to include a partial water change. Since algae consumes organic nutrients, harvesting the algae actually helps remove some of the organic load. The increased organic load can also be due to uneaten food accumulating in the aquarium. Pay attention to how much food your fish are actually eating and cut back on the amount if necessary.

Usually, cutting back on the number of hours per day the lights are on combined with a thorough cleaning will clear up the algae bloom. If these methods do not solve the problem, you probably have an excess of phosphate in your water and a phosphate filter media should be used. You may be tempted to use a commercial algaecide to get rid of the excess algae. This is actually a bad idea because these products often destroy the beneficial bacteria living in your filters. It is best to use natural methods to deal with the problem and refrain from adding chemicals to the aquarium unless they are absolutely necessary.

Maintaining The Aquarium

Chapter 15

MARINE FISH

This chapter will discuss many of the most common marine fish for sale in aquarium shops. The following pages will give you the basic information about these fish to include: what they look like, what conditions they prefer, what they eat, their temperament, and any other information that you need to know when determining which fish to include in your aquarium.

In order to understand some of the descriptions in this chapter as well as the information on marine fish diseases presented in Chapter 17, Marine Fish Diseases, it is important to understand the basic anatomy of a fish. Figure 10 shows a typical fish with the various body parts noted. Even though all basic fins are shown, it is important to note that not all of these fins exist on every species of fish.

At the top of each section of this chapter you will find the common name of a fish with the family name in parenthesis. This is followed by a picture of a representative member of the family along with its common name. Next is a description of the general characteristics of this family of fish. The last part of each section contains a description of specific members of the family. In this case, the common name is followed by the genus and species in parenthesis. Since some fish have several different common names, the family, genus, and species allow you to determine exactly which fish is being discussed. Finally, the typical maximum lengths that these fish can attain in the wild and in the aquarium is provided.

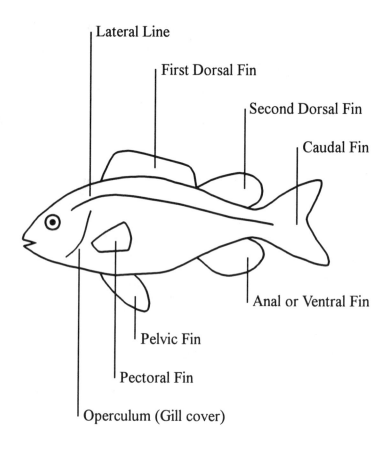

Figure 10. The basic anatomy of a fish.

ANGELFISH

(Family - Pomacanthidae)

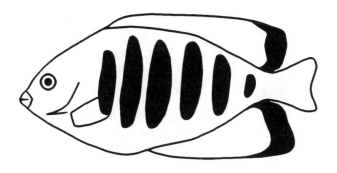

Flame Angelfish

Physical characteristics
These fish are oval in shape with a large variety of colors and markings. One distinguishing characteristic of angelfish is the spine on the gill cover that can be used for self defense. In the wild many members of this family can grow quite large, but some are suitable for the aquarium.

Temperament
Angelfish are territorial and do not tolerate each other or other fish very well. It is best to limit the number in an aquarium and to purchase them when they are young so that they have a better chance of acclimating to the aquarium.

These fish are also very sensitive to water quality. The smaller angelfish are compatible with invertebrates, but this is not the case for the larger members.

Feeding

In the wild angelfish eat smaller animals, algae, sponges and even coral. In the aquarium they need plenty of algae and will also take most live, meaty and frozen foods.

Common members of the angelfish family:

Flame Angelfish (*Centropyge loriculus*) - have bright red-orange bodies with several vertical black stripes. They can reach 4 inches in the wild and 3 inches in the aquarium.

Queen Angelfish (*Holacanthus ciliaris*) - are larger members of the family and have a yellowish body with some blue and green highlights, blue along the dorsal and ventral fins, and blue markings on the face. They can reach 18 inches in the wild and 12 inches in the aquarium.

Coral Beauty (*Centropyge bispinosus*) - these fish have purple bodies with yellow on the bottom that blends into the purple through many thin vertical stripes. They can reach 4 inches in the wild and 3 inches in the aquarium.

Rock Beauty (*Holacanthus tricolor*) - these are large yellow fish with a large dark area on their back half. These fish have a specialized diet that includes sponges and they usually do not survive long in captivity. They can reach 24 inches in the wild and 12 inches in the aquarium.

Marine Fish

Emperor Angelfish (*Pomacanthus imperator*) - are large yellow fish with many thin blue horizontal stripes and dark markings on the face and throat. As juveniles they are dark with whitish-blue concentric rings centered on the base of the caudal fin. They can reach 16 inches in the wild and 12 inches in the aquarium.

French Angelfish (*Pomacanthus paru*) - are large dark fish with many yellowish vertical specks on the sides and a grayish face. As juveniles they are dark with vertical yellow stripes. They can reach 12 inches in the wild and 8 inches in the aquarium.

Marine Fish

BATFISH

(Family - Platacidae)

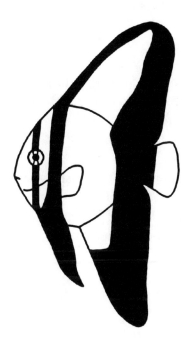

Batfish

Physical characteristics
These are large fish with oval shaped bodies and large rounded fins. The batfish grow quickly and since they are a "tall" fish they need a very tall aquarium to live in.

Temperament

Batfish are very peaceful and do well in a community tank. However, keep other aggressive fish away from them because their large fins make tempting targets. They are compatible with invertebrates.

Feeding

These fish are scavengers in the wild. Purchase young batfish that have been feeding in the store aquariums because some of them are slow to acclimate to aquarium food. In the aquarium, start feeding them live brine shrimp and eventually they will eat almost anything.

Common members of the batfish family:

Batfish (*Platax orbicularis*) - are dark brown in color with darker vertical bands. They can reach 20 inches in the wild and 12 inches in the aquarium.

BLENNIES

(Family - Blennidae)

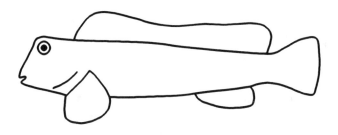

Bicolor Blenny

Physical characteristics

Blennies are small, elongated fish that often have their eyes located high on their blunt heads. Most have very plain coloration and markings; however, some are brightly colored.

Temperament

Most blennies are peaceful but somewhat territorial and need plenty of nooks and holes to make their home in. A few blennies are both territorial and aggressive and should not be kept with other members of the same species. If these aggressive blennies are kept with other species, their aquarium neighbors should be much larger. Blennies are very compatible with invertebrates.

Marine Fish

Feeding

Blennies take all kinds of food readily. The more aggressive members will even eat or bite their neighbors.

Common members of the blennie family:

Bicolor Blenny (*Ecsenius bicolor*) - these fish are brown/orange up front and red/orange on the back half. This is one of the more peaceful blennies. They can reach 4 inches in the wild and 3 inches in the aquarium.

Scooter Blenny (*Petrosciretes temmincki*) - these fish are black with white blotches and are one of the more peaceful blennies. They can reach 4 inches in the wild and 3 inches in the aquarium.

Midas Blenny (*Ecsenius midas*) - these fish are red/orange all over and are peaceful but territorial. They can reach 4 inches in the wild and 3 inches in the aquarium.

False Cleanerfish (*Aspidontus taeniatus*) - are silver up front blending to light blue in back with a horizontal black stripe starting at the mouth and extending all the way to the caudal fin. They also have a pointed head and look like a Cleaner Wrasse except that False Cleanerfish have an underslung mouth. The Cleaner Wrasse mouth comes to a point directly in front. This close resemblance to a Cleaner Wrasse allows the False Cleanerfish to get close to other fish and take unexpected bites. They are very aggressive and should not be kept with other fish. They can reach 4 inches in the wild and 3 inches in the aquarium.

Marine Fish

BUTTERFLYFISH

(Family - Chaetodontidae)

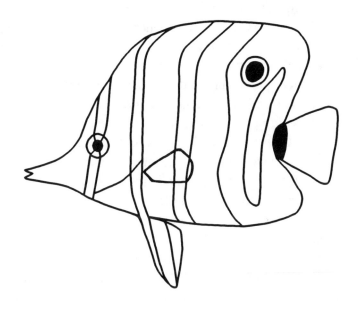

Copper-band Butterflyfish

Physical characteristics
Butterflyfish have very thin, oval shaped bodies that are well suited for life in a coral reef. They have bright colors and markings which serve to camouflage vital body parts and confuse predators. Butterflyfish typically have small, pointed mouths which allow them to pick food out of tight spaces. Some species of butterflyfish will grow from 6 to 9

inches in their natural habitat, but typically they only reach 3 to 4 inches in an aquarium.

Temperament

Butterflyfish are difficult to keep and are not recommended for the beginner. As a general rule, the more attractive and striking a butterflyfish is, the harder it is to keep. They prefer very good water quality, some have very particular food requirements, and they can become stressed when some aspect of life in an aquarium does not suit them. Most butterflyfish are peaceful but some may be very intolerant of members of their own family. It is best to purchase juvenile butterflyfish since they may acclimatize to aquarium life as they grow older. They are definitely not compatible with sessile invertebrates such as anemones or coral.

Feeding

These fish are grazers (as noted by the shape of their mouth) and their natural diet includes algae, coral, sponges, and small plankton. In the aquarium they are picky eaters but can be coaxed into eating live brine shrimp and high quality frozen foods. Be sure that you feed a large variety of foods and that the pieces are small enough for the butterflyfish's small mouth. Include algae and sponge based foods in their diet.

Common members of the butterflyfish family:

Copper-band Butterflyfish (*Chelmon rostratus*) - have yellow-orange vertical stripes with a very distinctive "false eye" on the rear of the dorsal fin to confuse predators. The long, slender mouth is very indicative of their feeding behavior in the coral reef. They can reach 6 inches in the wild and 4 inches in the aquarium.

Banded Butterflyfish (*Chaetodon striatus*) - are shaped like the Copper-band Butterflyfish except that the mouth is not as long. They have four dark vertical bands, one of which passes through the eye, and can reach 6 inches in the wild and 4 inches in the aquarium.

Black-banded Butterflyfish (*Chaetodon melannotus*) - are shaped like the Banded Butterflyfish but have numerous thin black bands that run diagonal from the lower front to the upper rear of the fish. They also have one vertical black band running through the eye and can reach 6 inches in the wild and 4 inches in the aquarium.

Raccoon Butterflyfish (*Chaetodon lunula*) - these are among the more hearty members of the family. They are dark yellow in color with a "false eye" on the rear of the dorsal fin, a dark vertical band running through the real eye, a white band just behind this dark band and finally one broad dark band extending diagonally from the gill up and back toward the dorsal fin. They can reach 8 inches in the wild and 5 inches in the aquarium.

Blue-striped Butterflyfish (*Chaetodon frembli*) - are yellowish in color with thin blue horizontal stripes and a large dark spot at the base of the caudal fin. They can reach 8 inches in the wild and 5 inches in the aquarium.

Marine Fish

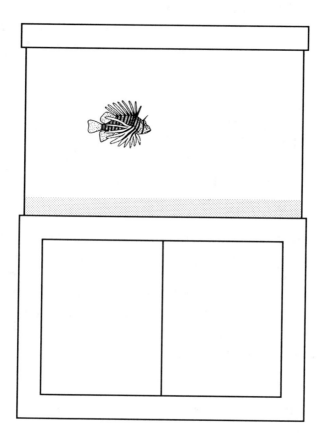

CARDINALFISH

(Family - Apogonidae)

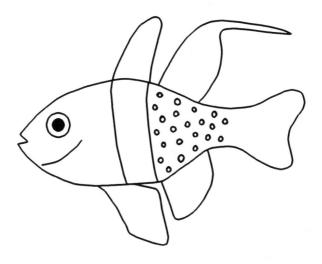

Pajama Cardinalfish

Physical characteristics

A characteristic of these fish is the large head and two dorsal fins. Some of them can reach lengths of 4 to 6 inches in their natural environment. In captivity, however, they only reach 3 inches.

Temperament

They are hardy fish that do well in a community

aquarium. Most species are nocturnal and like to hide out between the rocks and coral heads during the day. They are normally slow moving and not aggressive and can lose out in the competition for food if the aquarium has larger, more aggressive fish. These fish get along well with invertebrates.

Feeding
Cardinalfish prefer live foods but will accept most other kinds except flake.

Common members of the cardinalfish family:
Pajama Cardinalfish (*Sphaeramia nematopterus*) - are gray to yellow in color with one vertical black band down the body from the first dorsal fin and numerous reddish dots on the back half of the fish. These dots resemble pajama bottoms and gave these fish their name. Unlike most other cardinalfish, Pajama Cardinalfish are active during the day. They can reach 4 inches in the wild and 3 inches in the aquarium.

Flamefish (*Apogon maculatus*) - are somewhat more streamlined than the Pajama Cardinalfish and are red with two horizontal white stripes on each eye. They also have a dark patch below the second dorsal fin and another at the base of the tail. They can reach 6 inches in the wild and 3 inches in the aquarium.

Marine Fish

CLOWNFISH

(Family - Pomacentridae)

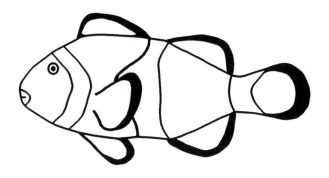

Percula Clown

Physical characteristics

The Pomacentridae family actually consists of two distinct types of fish: the clownfish (sometimes referred to as the anemonefish) and the damselfish. Because these two types have different characteristics, they will each be covered individually with the damselfish discussed later in this chapter. Clownfish are brightly colored and swim with an unusual motion giving rise to their common name. These fish typically live in a mutually beneficial relationship with anemones. The clownfish help provide protection and food for the anemone and in turn gain protection for themselves by hiding in the stinging tentacles of the anemone. Clownfish are imune to the stings of the anemone tentacles.

Marine Fish

Temperament

Clownfish are generally peaceful; however, some individuals can be aggressive, especially as they grow older. Unless your aquarium is very large, it is best to keep a single anemonefish or a mated pair. Otherwise, territorial battles are likely to break out. Clownfish do well with or without a host anemone. Keep in mind, though, that an anemone requires specialized equipment and techniques and should not be attempted until an advanced level of experience and knowledge is gained. All clownfish are compatible with invertebrates.

Feeding

The natural diet of clownfish consists of small, live animals. They are aggressive eaters and will readily take live, frozen, meaty, and vegetable based foods in the aquarium.

Common members of the anemonefish family:

Percula Clown (*Amphiprion ocellaris*) - these fish are the most commonly recognized clownfish. They are reddish orange with white bands and black trim around the fins and can reach 3 inches in the wild and in the aquarium.

Tomato Clown (*Amphiprion frenatus* and *ephippium*) - these fish are tomato red and may or may not have a single vertical white band behind the eyes. Actually the name tomato clown is applied to two different species of anemonefish. One species (*Amphiprion frenatus*) has the white band all through life and the other species (*Amphiprion ephippium*) only has the with band when it is young. *Amphiprion frenatus* can reach 3 inches in the wild and 2 inches in the aquarium.

Marine Fish

Amphiprion ephippium can reach 4 inches in the wild and 3 inches in the aquarium.

Salmon Clownfish (*Amphiprion perideraion*) - are pale orange or salmon colored with one thin vertical band behind the eyes. They can reach 3 inches in the wild and 2 inches in the aquarium.

Marine Fish

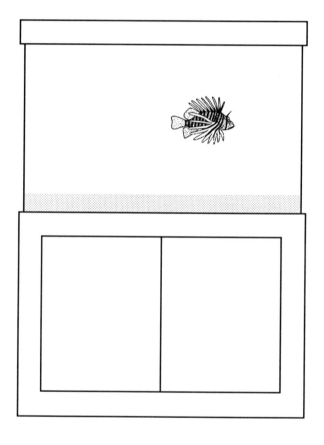

DAMSELFISH

(Family - Pomacentridae)

Domino Damsel

Physical characteristics

This is the other member, along with the anemonefish described earlier, of the Pomacentridae family. Damsel-fish are hardy, robust, fast moving, and aggressive fish. Because they are so hardy, they are often used to start the nitrogen cycle in a new aquarium. However, once the nitrogen cycle is completed, the aquarist will have a very aggressive fish in the aquarium that may not be very compatible with any other fish. Damselfish vary widely in color and either have an oval or a more elongated shape.

Temperament
Most damselfish are very aggressive and will harass other members of their family and members of other families. They are compatible with invertebrates.

Feeding
The natural diet of the damselfish consists of small, live food. In the aquarium they will readily eat all kinds of live and frozen foods.

Common members of the damselfish family:
Domino Damsel (*Dascyllus trimaculatus*) - these fish are all black except for a white spot on the forehead and one white spot on each side below the middle of the dorsal fin. They can reach 5 inches in the wild and 3 inches in the aquarium.

White-tailed Damselfish (*Dascyllus aruanus*) - are shaped like the Domino Damsel and are white in color with three vertical black bands and a white tail. They can reach 4 inches in the wild and 3 inches in the aquarium.

Black-tailed Damselfish (*Dascyllus melanurus*) - look like the White-tailed Damselfish except that the tail is black. They can reach 3 inches in the wild and in the aquarium.

Sergeant Major (*Abudefduf saxatilis*) - these fish are

also shaped like the Domino Damsel but are silvery in color with some yellow below the dorsal fin and five vertical black stripes. They can reach 6 inches in the wild and 3 inches in the aquarium.

Yellow-tailed Damselfish (*Chromis xanthurus*) - are somewhat elongated and blue in color with a yellow caudal fin. They can reach 4 inches in the wild and 2 inches in the aquarium.

Blue Damsel (*Abudefduf cyaneus*) - are elongated and electric blue in color and may have some yellow on the ventral and caudal fin. They can reach 3 inches in the wild and 2 inches in the aquarium.

Blue Chromis (*Chromis cyanea*) - are elongated and blue with a black stripe running along the top of the body below the dorsal fin. They are peaceful fish that can be kept in a community aquarium and prefer to be with some members of their own family. They can reach 2 inches in the wild and in the aquarium.

Green Chromis (*Chromis caerulea*) - are elongated and bluish green in color. They are peaceful fish that can be kept in a community aquarium and prefer to be with some members of their own family. They can reach 4 inches in the wild and 2 inches in the aquarium.

Marine Fish

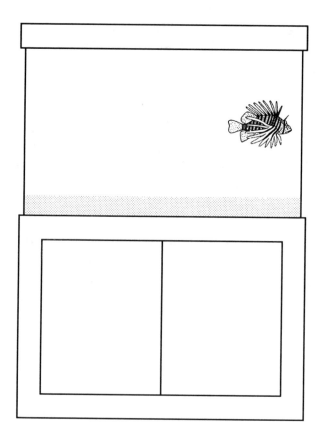

FILEFISH

(Family - Monocanthidae)

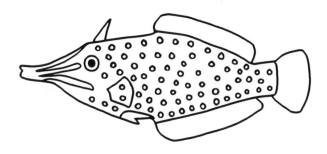

Long-nosed Filefish

Physical characteristics

Filefish share many characteristics with the triggerfish family, Balistidae, and are sometimes classified in that family. These fish have an elongated diamond-shaped body and are typically very thin. Like the triggerfish, the first dorsal fin of the filefish can be raised and locked in place or lowered when not needed. In their natural habitat some filefish can reach up to 24 inches in length, but some are much smaller and suitable for the aquarium.

Temperament

Filefish are generally peaceful and less active than triggerfish. They are sometimes shy and withdrawn when first introduced into an aquarium. With time they will settle in and make a good neighbor in a community tank. They are not compatible with invertebrates.

Feeding

These fish have tiny mouths, and their natural diet consists of coral polyps and algae. Given their shy, less active behavior and a lack of their natural foods, filefish sometimes do not get enough to eat when first introduced into the aquarium. They will require special attention during this time, and live brine shrimp may help the transition. Eventually they will learn to accept most marine foods.

Common members of the filefish family:

Long-nosed Filefish (*Oxymonacanthus longirostris*) - are brightly colored with a greenish body and yellow spots and fins. They can reach 4 inches in the wild and 3 inches in the aquarium.

Fantail Filefish (*Pervagor spilosoma*) - are similar to the Long-nosed Filefish but have a grayish-white body with dark spots. They can reach 6 inches in the wild and 5 inches in the aquarium.

GOBIES

(Family - Gobiidae)

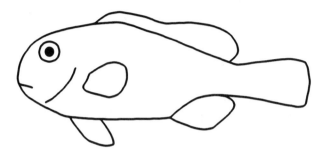

Yellow Goby

Physical characteristics

Gobies are small bottom-dwelling fish with elongated bodies and blunt heads. They are similar to many blennies, but tend to have brighter colors.

Temperament

These are peaceful fish, however, they do not tolerate other members of their family very well and should be kept individually. They make good additions to a community aquarium and like to have plenty of places to perch. They are compatible with invertebrates.

Feeding

Their natural foods include small crustaceans and

other small live foods. In the aquarium they prefer live foods but will take frozen foods.

Common members of the goby family:
Yellow Goby (*Gobiodon okinawae*) - these fish are completely yellow. They are among the smaller gobies, reaching only 1 inch long in the wild and in the aquarium.

Lemon Goby (*Gobiodon citrinus*) - these fish are very similar to the Yellow Goby except they are reddish-orange with a few thin blue stripes around the head and at the base of the dorsal and anal fins. They can reach 1 inch in the wild and in the aquarium.

Catalina Goby (*Lythrypnus dalli*) - these fish are more elongated than the Yellow Goby and larger. They are red with thin vertical blue stripes and can reach 2 inches in the wild and in the aquarium.

GRAMMAS

(Family - Grammidae)

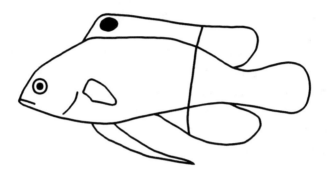

Royal Gramma

Physical characteristics

These elongated, colorful fish are also know as fairy basslets and are closely related to the pygmy basslets (Pseudochromidae).

Temperament

Grammas are generally peaceful and require lots of places to retreat to. They do not tolerate other members of their own family very well, and some can be very territorial. They are well suited for invertebrates.

Feeding

In the wild they eat small, live foods. In the aquarium

they will eat most live and frozen foods.

Common members of the gramma family:
Royal Gramma (*Gramma loreto*) - these fish are purple up front blending into an orange tail. They can reach 5 inches in the wild and 3 inches in the aquarium.

Black Cap Gramma (*Gramma melacara*) - these fish are shaped like the Royal Gramma but are purple in color with a black streak running from the top of its head and along the top of the dorsal fin. They are extremely territorial and can be aggressive. They can reach 4 inches in the wild and 3 inches in the aquarium.

HAWKFISH

(Family - Cirrhitidae)

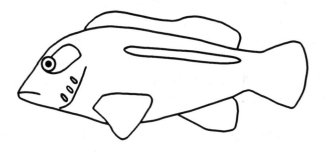

Arc Eye Hawkfish

Physical characteristics

Hawkfish vary from elongated to very elongated. An interesting characteristic of these fish is the highly developed pectoral fin which they sometimes use as a limb to "walk" along the bottom or across a rock.

Temperament

Hawkfish are peaceful and can be kept with other members of their own family. They are generally slow moving except when disturbed or eating. Most of the time they like to perch on rocks observing the world and watching for food to float by. They eat invertebrates in the wild, but are compatible with them in the aquarium.

Marine Fish

Feeding

Their natural foods are small invertebrates and small fish. In the aquarium they are content with live foods and meaty frozen foods.

Common members of the hawkfish family:

Arc Eye Hawkfish (*Paracirrhites arcatus*) - are reddish-brown to reddish-gray with a white horizontal stripe. The distinguishing characteristic is the reddish-orange arc extending behind and above each eye. They can reach 5 inches in the wild and 4 inches in the aquarium.

Scarlet Hawkfish (*Neocirrhites armatus*) - are bright red with a black streak under the dorsal fin. They can reach 3 inches in the wild and 2 inches in the aquarium.

Long-nosed Hawkfish (*Oxycirrhites typus*) - are very elongated with a milky body and red cross hatched markings. The mouth is long and pointed. They can reach 4 inches in the wild and 3 inches in the aquarium.

JAWFISH

(Family - Opistognathidae)

Yellow-headed Jawfish

Physical characteristics

Jawfish are long, slender fish with a somewhat jutting lower jaw. They build burrows in the bottom substrate in which to retreat for safety and tend to spend much of their time in a head up, tail down swimming posture.

Marine Fish

Temperament

Since these fish are burrow builders, they need a suitably thick bottom substrate (several inches). This burrowing behavior is quite fascinating. They are peaceful around other species, but will only tolerate other members of their family if they have a lot of space for themselves and do not feel crowded. They are also compatible with invertebrates.

Feeding

Jawfish prefer small, live foods, but will also eat small pieces of chopped fish, squid or clam. They will also eat live brine shrimp.

Common members of the jawfish family:

Yellow-headed Jawfish (*Opistognathus aurifrons*) - have a yellow head that slowly blends into a blue tail and fins. They can reach 5 inches in the wild and 3 inches in the aquarium.

LIONFISH

(Family - Scorpaenidae)

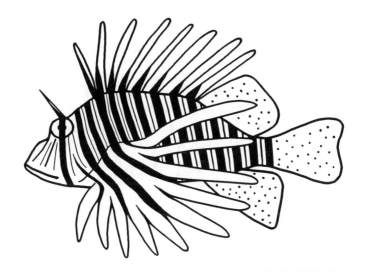

Lionfish

Physical characteristics
   Lionfish are very striking and exotic fish. They have large, elaborate pectoral fins and the dorsal fins contain hollow spines connected to poison sacs that can inflict painful and even fatal wounds. Therefore, these fish need to be handled with great respect.

Temperament
   These fish are generally peaceful and hang majesti-

cally in the mid-water. This slow motion often entices divers to try to touch the fish, resulting in a handful of puncture wounds from the spines. In the aquarium they will not attack unless they are provoked. If you stay aware of where they are and do not harass them, they can be make good additions to your aquarium.

Feeding
Their natural food is small fish, and in the aquarium any fish that is much smaller than the lionfish is at risk. However, it is possible to keep them well fed with live brine shrimp and frozen or prepared meaty foods so that they do not bother the smaller fish. Their eating behavior is noteworthy. They have a very large mouth which they open quickly, sucking the food in. So, while hanging motionless in the water, any food that passes within range can disappear in an instant.

Common members of the lionfish family:
Lionfish (*Pterois volitans*) - are covered with thin, vertical stripes alternating between white and reddish-brown. The pelvic, anal, and caudal fins are mostly transparent. They can reach 14 inches in the wild and 8 inches in the aquarium.

Scorpionfish (*Pterois antennata*) - are very similar to the Lionfish except that the reddish-brown vertical stripes are wider. They can reach 10 inches in the wild and 6 inches in the aquarium.

White-fin Lionfish (*Pterois radiata*) - are similar to the Scorpionfish except that the reddish-brown stripes are even wider, and the pectoral and dorsal fins have white stripes.

They can reach 10 inches in the wild and 6 inches in the aquarium.

Turkeyfish (*Dendrochirus brachypterus*) - are similar to the White-fin Lionfish except that the dorsal and pectoral fins are not as long and do not have the white stripe. The webbing on the pectoral fins is also more fully developed. They can reach 6 inches in the wild and 4 inches in the aquarium.

Marine Fish

MANDARINFISH

(Family - Callionymidae)

Mandarinfish

Physical characteristics
These are small, elongated fish with extremely bold colors and markings. Mandarinfish are sometimes called by the name Dragonets, which is a related species.

Temperament
Mandarinfish are peaceful if kept singly or as a mated pair. They will not tolerate other members of their own family. These fish are shy and like lots of places to perch close to the bottom of the aquarium. Mandarinfish arc vcry compatible with invertebrates.

Marine Fish

Feeding

In the wild these fish eat small animals and crustaceans on the ocean floor. In the aquarium they require occasional small, live food such as young brine shrimp. They also eat algae and will take many other kinds of frozen and prepared food. They are shy eaters and can lose out in competition for food with a lot of aggressive eaters.

Common members of the mandarinfish family:

Mandarinfish (*Synchiropus splendidus*) - are basically greenish with bold red-orange and blue markings. They can reach 4 inches in the wild and 3 inches in the aquarium.

Psychedelic Fish (*Synchiropus picturatus*) - are very similar in size and shape to the Mandarinfish. However, the Psychedelic Fish have dark green patches with redish, black and green borders on an otherwise greenish body. They can reach 4 inches in the wild and 3 inches in the aquarium.

MOORISH IDOL

(Family - Zanclidae)

Moorish Idol

Physical characteristics
Moorish Idols have a very thin, oval-shaped bodies with an elaborate dorsal fin that trails off well above and behind the caudal fin.

Temperament
Moorish Idols are a peaceful fish that adapt very poorly to captivity. In the aquarium they generally do not eat much, if any, food of any kind and become weak and very prone to disease. As a result, they will not live long. They

are a very handsome fish and you may find them in many aquarium shops. A very experienced aquarist may be able to successfully keep them, but in general, they are better off left in the ocean.

Feeding

Moorish Idols appear to need a wide variety of foods. In the aquarium they seem to prefer small, live crustaceans and plenty of algae.

The only member of the Moorish Idol family:

Moorish Idol (*Zanclus canescens*) - these fish have bold black bands across a yellow body that fades into white at the head and fins. They can reach 6 inches in the wild and 4 inches in the aquarium.

MORAY EELS

(Family - Muraenidae)

Snowflake Moray

Physical characteristics

Moray eels have very long bodies somewhat like a thick snake. They do not have any pectoral fins, and the dorsal fin extends the entire length of the body and blends into the caudal fin. They breathe by rhythmically opening and closing the mouth forcing water over the gills. Moray eels can reach 5 to 6 feet long in the wild, and it is not unusual for them to reach 2 to 3 feet in an aquarium.

Temperament

Moray eels have a reputation as being dangerous fish. While some members of the family deserve this reputation, most are shy and will only attack when provoked. Normally they are seen hiding in holes in a reef with only their heads sticking out. Most fish and crustaceans that share an aquarium with a moray eel will be at risk. You can minimize a depletion of your prized animals by keeping the moray well fed.

Feeding

Moray eels like fish, crabs, and other live crustaceans. You can entice them to eat a chunk of prepared, meaty fish by holding it in a long pair of forceps and waving it gently in front of them. Morays have been known to chase their food onto the beach or on top of an exposed coral head. Many aquarists have even found them on the floor many feet from the aquarium. So, keep a good, tight cover on an aquarium with a moray eel inside.

Common member of the moray eel family:

Snowflake Moray (*Echnida nebulosa*) - these fish are basically white with black blotches all over their bodies. These markings actually take on a look of large snowflakes, accounting for the name. They can reach 36 inches in the wild and 24 inches in the aquarium.

PORCUPINEFISH

(Family - Diodontidae)

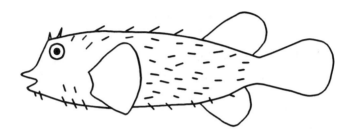

Spiney Boxfish

Physical characteristics

The bodies of porcupinefish are covered with spines, and these fish have the ability to inflate themselves when threatened. The inflated fish with the extended spines is the source of the common name. Many people try to make these fish inflate for amusement; however, this is very stressful for the porcupinefish and should not be done. The largest members of this family can reach up to 24 to 36 inches in length, but considerably less in the aquarium.

Temperament

Porcupinefish are typically aggressive towards other members of their family as well as smaller fish of other families. They are also not suited for invertebrates.

Marine Fish

Feeding

In the wild porcupinefish eat crustaceans and small fish. They are aggressive feeders in the aquarium and will take most meaty foods.

Common members of the porcupinefish family:

Spiny Boxfish (*Chilomycterus schoepfi*) - are yellowish with brown markings that make a net-like pattern. They can reach 12 inches in the wild and 4 inches in the aquarium.

Long-spined Porcupinefish (*Diodon holacanthus*) - have a brownish body with small dark spots and long spines. They can reach 18 inches in the wild and 6 inches in the aquarium.

Common Porcupinefish (*Diodon hystrix*) - are similar to the Long-spined Porcupine fish except they have shorter spines. These fish are more peaceful around other fish than most porcupinefish. They can reach 24 inches in the wild and 8 inches in the aquarium.

PSEUDOCHROMIS

(Family - Pseudochromidae)

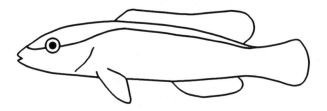

Flash-back Gramma

Physical characteristics

These elongated, colorful fish are also known as pygmy basslets. They are closely related to the Gramma family (*Grammidae*) and the name "Gramma" often appears in the common names of these fish. They are small fish reaching 2 to 3 inches in the wild and approximately the same length in an aquarium.

Temperament

Pseudochromis are generally peaceful and require lots of places to retreat to. They do not tolerate other members of their own family very well, and some can be very territorial. They are well suited for invertebrates.

Feeding

In the wild they eat small crustaceans. In the aquarium they will eat most live and frozen foods.

Marine Fish

Common members of the pseudochromis family:

Flash-back Gramma (*Pseudochromis diadema*) - these fish are yellow with a purple streak running along the back from the head almost to the tail. They can reach 2 inches in the wild and in the aquarium.

Neon-back Gramma (*Pseudochromis dutoiti*) - these fish are shaped much like a Flash-back Gramma except that they are more orange in color with a blue streak along the back and blue markings on the face. They can reach 3 inches in the wild and 2 to 3 inches in the aquarium.

Strawberry Gramma (*Pseudochromis porphyreus*) - these fish are shaped like the Flash-back Gramma; however, they are totally reddish-purple in color. They can reach 2 inches in the wild and in the aquarium.

PUFFERS

(Family - Tetraodontidae)

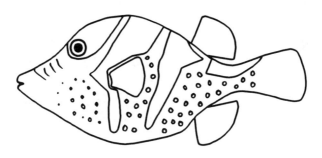

Black-saddled Puffer

Physical characteristics

These fish are smooth skinned and have the ability to inflate themselves when threatened. As with the porcupine-fish, the puffer should not be harassed into inflating itself since this is stressful for the fish. Puffers have very prominent teeth which are actually fused bone. Larger members of the family can reach up to 20 inches in the wild.

Temperament

Puffers are generally peaceful except that they do not tolerate other members of their own family very well. Because they are slow moving they sometimes get harassed by other more aggressive fish. They are not at all compatible with invertebrates.

Feeding
They eat small fish and crustaceans in the wild and will eat meaty foods in the aquarium.

Common members of the puffer family:
Black-saddled Puffer (*Canthigaster valentini*) - these fish are cream colored with dark patches on the back and light brown spots on the lower half. They are some of the smaller pufferfish and can reach 8 inches in the wild and 3 inches in the aquarium.

Sharp-nosed Puffer (*Canthigaster solandri*) - these fish are yellow-brown on the bottom and brown on top with white spots lengthwise along the midline turning into blue lines on top. They are also some of the smaller puffers and can reach 4 inches in the wild and 2 inches in the aquarium.

SEAHORSES

(Family - Syngnathidae)

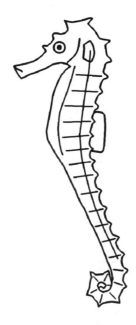

Florida Seahorse

Physical characteristics

Seahorses are slow moving fish that swim in an upright, head higher than the tail, manner. They have plate-like scales that are fused into a hard but flexible skin. Seahorses do not have a caudal fin, instead they have a prehensile tail that is used to grasp objects for stability. They reach 6 to 10 inches in the wild and somewhat less in an aquarium.

Marine Fish

Temperament

Seahorses are very peaceful and need to have peaceful aquarium neighbors. They are very sensitive to water conditions and suffer when water quality is less than excellent. They are very compatible with invertebrates.

Feeding

In the wild these fish eat very small live animals and plankton. In the aquarium these slow moving fish often do not get enough to eat because they lose out in the competition for food with faster fish. So, it is best to keep seahorses in their own aquarium. They do very well with small live brine shrimp and other small, live foods. They will take frozen foods, such as brine shrimp, only as a last resort.

Common members of the seahorse family:

Florida Seahorse (*Hippocampus erectus*) - these fish are yellowish-brown in color or even gray or red. They can reach 6 inches in the wild and 4 to 5 inches in the aquarium.

Yellow Seahorse (*Hippocampus kuda*) - these fish are very similar to the Florida Seahorse but are larger and tend to be more yellow in color. They can reach 10 inches in the wild and 6 to 8 inches in the aquarium.

SURGEONS and TANGS

(Family - Acanthuridae)

Yellow Tang

Physical characteristics

This popular family is known by the common name of tang or surgeon fish. They get this name because of a small sharp spine at the base of the caudal fin. This spine can be erected at will and used as a defense mechanism. Tangs and surgeons are typically oval in shape with thin brightly colored bodies and large dorsal and anal fins.

Temperament

Tangs and surgeon fish are usually peaceful in a community aquarium provided they have plenty of room to swim

Marine Fish

around. If they are crowded they will often fight amongst themselves. They will also fight with each other whenever a new member of their family is introduced into the aquarium. It is best to introduce these fish when they are young and let them grow up together. If an older fish is to be added to the aquarium, it is usually better to introduce larger rather than smaller members so that the new fish will be able to defend itself better. These fish are usually compatible with invertebrates.

Feeding

They take most foods readily; however, they are grazers and absolutely require an abundant growth of algae, blanched leafy green vegetables, or prepared foods high in algae or vegetable content.

Common members of the tang and surgeon family:

Yellow Tang (*Zebrasoma flavescens*) - these fish live up to their name by being all yellow. They can reach 8 inches in the wild and 4 to 6 inches in the aquarium.

Blue Tang (*Acanthurus coeruleus*) - these fish are shaped like a Yellow Tang however they are blue in color. Juvenile Blue Tangs are yellow and turn blue with age. They can reach 12 inches in the wild and 6 inches in the aquarium.

Sailfin Tang (*Zebrasoma veliferum*) - these fish are shaped like the Yellow Tang, but have much larger fins and are mostly brown with several thin white to yellow vertical bands. They can reach 15 inches in the wild and 8 inches in the aquarium.

Marine Fish

Convict Tang (*Acanthurus triostegus*) - these fish are shaped like a Yellow Tang; however, they are gray/silver with thin vertical black stripes. They can reach 9 inches in the wild and 4 inches in the aquarium.

Regal Tang (*Paracanthurus hepatus*) - also known as Blue Surgeon, have a shape that is somewhat streamlined when compared to a Yellow Tang. They are mostly blue with black markings on the body and a yellow tail. They can reach 10 inches in the wild and 4 to 6 inches in the aquarium.

Achilles Tang (*Acanthurus achilles*) - also know as Red-tailed Surgeon, are shaped somewhat like a Yellow Tang and are mostly black with orange markings at the base of the tail and on the tail itself. They can reach 10 inches in the wild and 7 to 8 inches in the aquarium.

Powder Blue Surgeon (*Acanthurus leucosternon*) - these fish have a more streamlined shape and a powder blue body. They also have a black face and a yellow dorsal fin. They can reach 10 inches in the wild and 7 to 8 inches in the aquarium.

Clown Surgeon (*Acanthurus lineatus*) - these fish have the more streamlined shape with a yellow to orange body with blue horizontal stripes. They can reach 11 inches in the wild and 6 inches in the aquarium.

Kole Tang (*Ctenochaetus strigosus*) - these fish are shaped like the Yellow Tang but are dark purple with thin horizontal stripes that are very light yellow giving an overall brownish-purple color. The eyes are ringed with yellow, and all the fins have a light yellow tint making them a very striking fish. They can reach 8 inches in the wild and 4 to 6 inches in the aquarium.

Marine Fish

TRIGGERFISH

(Family - Balistidae)

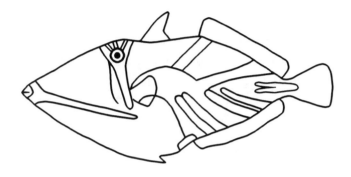

Picasso Trigger

Physical characteristics

The Triggerfish family received that name because of a mechanism that allows the first dorsal fin to be either lowered or raised and locked into place. By raising the fin the triggerfish can secure itself in a crevice for protection. This family is usually quite colorful with striking markings; however, some members are very plain. These fish have powerful jaws and sharp teeth that allow them to eat invertebrates. In their natural habitat various members of this family can grow up to 20 inches long. In an aquarium they can reach 6 to 10 inches in length.

Temperament

Triggerfish are typically aggressive and do not tolerate other members of the same species very well. Some triggerfish may also pick on smaller members of other species. These fish are definitely not compatible with invertebrates.

Feeding

Triggerfish have robust appetites and will readily take all kinds of food. They particularly like invertebrates and are not even deterred by sea urchin spines. If spines or thorns get in the way, the triggerfish simply turns the invertebrate over by directing a squirt of water underneath the victim and eats the soft, unprotected parts.

Common members of the triggerfish family:

Picasso Trigger (*Rhinecanthus aculeatus*) - these fish are yellowish on top and white underneath. In the middle of each side is a dark spot with bright yellow, white, and dark stripes emanating out from it. Across the forehead between the eyes are alternating blue and dark stripes. They can reach 12 inches in the wild and 9 inches in the aquarium.

Queen Trigger (*Balistes vetula*) - these fish are yellowish along the back and white on the ventral side with blue markings on the fins and around the mouth. They also have dark lines radiating out from the eyes and can reach 12 inches in the wild and 9 inches in the aquarium.

Clown Trigger (*Balistoides conspicillum*) - these fish are mostly dark with large white spots on the lower body. They also have a yellow patch on the mouth and near the first dorsal fin. These fish can reach 20 inches in the wild and 10 inches in the aquarium.

Black Triggerfish (*Odonus niger*) - have a solid dark color that ranges from dark blue to dark green. They can reach 20 inches in the wild and 10 inches in the aquarium.

Rectangular Triggerfish (*Rhinecanthus rectangulus*) - (also known as Lagoon Triggerfish) have a broad dark band running diagonally from the eyes to the anal fin. They are also identified by markings pointing forward from the base of the second dorsal fin and the anal fin. These markings join each other forming a point like an arrowhead pointing toward the mid body. They can reach 10 inches in the wild and 8 inches in the aquarium.

Marine Fish

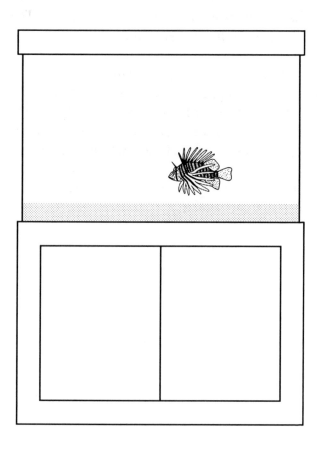

WRASSES

(Family - Labridae)

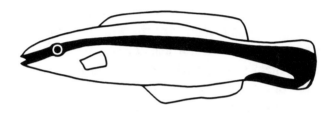

Cleaner Wrasse

Physical characteristics
　　The wrasse family has many different members; they are hardy, elongated fish with bright colors and markings. They typically only use the pectoral fins for swimming and rely on the caudal fin for directional control.

Temperament
　　In general, wrasses are peaceful and make good additions to a community tank. They have a great variety of characteristics such as: some perform cleaning duties on other fish, some spin cocoons to sleep in, and others burrow into the sand for long periods of time. In the wild the larger varieties can reach 12 to 24 inches long. In the aquarium the largest varieties will reach 6 to 12 inches with many of the other

varieties reaching 3 to 6 inches. The smaller wrasses are compatible with invertebrates, but can become increasingly incompatible as they grow larger. It is also not a good idea to keep small fish around the larger wrasses.

Feeding

In their natural environment wrasses eat mollusks and crustaceans. Some members of the wrasse family are commonly known as parrotfish which have hard beak like mouths that allow them to bite off hunks of coral from which they digest the polyps and excrete the rest as coral sand. In the aquarium wrasses will eat brine shrimp, meaty foods, and most frozen foods.

Common members of the wrasse family:

Cleaner Wrasse (*Labroides dimidiatus*) - these fish are very elongated, silvery up front and blue to the back with a horizontal black stripe running from the mouth to the tail. These fish clean parasites from other fish while swimming around and through their gills and mouth, a behavior that is beneficial and readily tolerated. They are often confused with the undesirable False Cleanerfish which was discussed in the Blennie section of this chapter. The mouth will reveal the difference. The Cleaner Wrasse head comes to a point with the mouth directly on the end, good for picking. The False Cleanerfish have an underslung mouth. The Cleaner Wrasse can reach 4 inches in the wild and 3 inches in the aquarium.

Clown Wrasse (*Coris gaimardi*) - these are some of the longer wrasses. They are elongated and orange with white spots along the back when young. As they mature they turn

Marine Fish

brownish with blue spots along the body and an orange head. The tail is yellow. They can reach 12 inches in the wild and 6 inches in the aquarium.

Birdmouth Wrasse (*Gomphosus caeruleus*) - these are another of the larger wrasses. They are blue-green with a long pointed mouth that make them adept at picking food. They can reach 10 inches in the wild and 5 inches in the aquarium.

Banana Wrasse (*Halichoeres chrysus*) - these fish are elongated but small and yellow with light green markings on the face. They can reach 4 inches in the wild and 3 inches in the aquarium.

Spanish Hogfish (*Bodianus rufus*) - are very large members of the family and are mostly yellow with blue on the front upper half of the body and dorsal fin. They can reach 24 inches in the wild and 8 inches in the aquarium.

Cuban Hogfish (*Bodianus pulchellus*) - are large and elongated and mostly reddish-brown with a white horizontal stripe running from the mouth most of the way to the tail which is yellow. They can reach 10 inches in the wild and 6 inches in the aquarium.

Dwarf Parrot Wrasse (*Cirrhilabrus rubriventralis*) - these are small and colored orange with white on the ventral side. The fins have blue spots on them. They can reach 3 inches in the wild and 2 inches in the aquarium

Marine Fish

Green Parrot Wrasse (*Thalassoma lunare*) - also known as Green Parrotfish, are large and iridescent green with red and blue markings especially on the face. These fish make a mucous cocoon for protection while they sleep. They can reach 13 inches in the wild and 8 inches in the aquarium.

Chapter 16

INVERTEBRATES

This chapter will discuss the major types of marine invertebrates commonly found in saltwater aquarium shops. The following pages will give you the basic information to include what they look like, what they eat, their temperament, and other information that you need to know when determining which ones to add to your aquarium.

All fish belong to the phylum Pisces. This makes it possible to identify fish according to family name in the preceding chapter. Marine invertebrates on the other hand belong to many different phylum, so, it is common practice to identify them according to phylum rather than family. In this chapter you will find the common name of the invertebrate followed by the phylum name in parenthesis at the top of each section. Next is a picture of a representative member of the phylum along with its common name. Following this is a description of the general characteristics of this phylum and the last part of each section is a description of specific members. As in the previous chapter, the common name is followed by the genus and species in parenthesis to aid in specific identification.

You will note that many different kinds of invertebrates are not covered in this chapter. These invertebrates are excluded because they require special equipment, knowl-

Invertebrates

edge and techniques to keep them alive and healthy in an aquarium environment. Among these are anemones, clams, macro algaes, and hard and soft corals. Chapter 18, Introduction to Mini-Reefs, will discuss this subject further.

Invertebrates

CRABS

(Phylum - Crustacea)

Red Hermit Crab

Physical characteristics

Crabs have hard, rounded or angular bodies with walking legs along the sides and claws in front. Hermit crabs have an elongated body that is heavily armored except for the posterior which is very soft and is inserted in abandoned shells for protection. Crabs range from 1 inch long to well over 6 inches.

Temperament

Most small crabs make good additions to an aquarium. The exception here is the Fiddler Crab which can be aggressive and is not suited for a community aquarium. Any crab more than 1 or 2 inches long may be a little feisty and harass other fish in the aquarium.

Invertebrates

Feeding

Crabs are scavengers by nature and consume bits of food they find on the ocean floor. In the aquarium they will eat fresh and frozen, meaty foods.

Common crabs:

Red Hermit Crab (*Dardanus megistos*) - these crabs are red with small white dots. Since they can adopt any discarded shell for a home, the color, size, and shape of the shell varies greatly. They can reach 2-3 inches in the wild and in the aquarium.

Arrow Crab (*Stenorhynchus seticornis*) - these crabs have small, triangular, yellow and brown stripped bodies with very long legs. They will fight with their own kind so it is best to keep just one. They can reach up to 6 inches long including the legs.

Invertebrates

LOBSTERS

(Phylum - Crustacea)

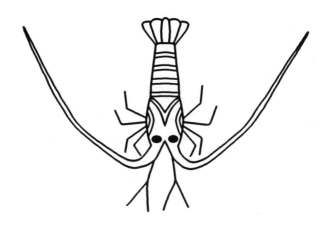

Purple Spiny Lobster

Physical characteristics

Lobsters are large, elongated crustaceans with walking legs and a muscular tail with a fin for rapid propulsion. They have very long antenna to help them sense the environment. Lobsters can reach lengths of 12 inches or more in the wild, and species suited for the aquarium can reach up to 8 inches.

Temperament

Most lobsters are peaceful and shy and, since they are nocturnal, they will spend the day hiding among the rocks

Invertebrates

at the bottom. However, as they become more acclimated to aquarium life, some lobsters will be seen out during the day.

Feeding
    Lobsters are scavengers and consume bits of food they find on the ocean floor. In the aquarium they will eat fresh and frozen meaty foods.

Common lobsters:
    Purple Spiny Lobster (*Panulirus versicolor*) - these lobsters are blue to purple in color with white antennas, white tail, and thin, white bands and stripes on the body. They can reach up to 8 inches in length.

    Red Dwarf Lobster (*Enoplometopus occidentalis*) - these lobsters are totally red with large well developed claws. They can reach up to 5 inches in length.

Invertebrates

SEA URCHINS

(Phylum - Echinodermata)

Rock-boring Urchin

Physical characteristics

Sea urchins have rounded, hard bodies covered with pointed spines. Depending on the species these spines can either be long or short, thick or thin. Including the spines, the largest sea urchins can reach diameters of almost 12 inches in the wild.

Temperament

These are peaceful grazers that make good additions to a community aquarium. Sea urchins can demonstrate a lot of power as they crawl around the aquarium and can easily topple over small- and medium-sized rocks.

Invertebrates

Feeding

Sea urchins are herbivores and require an abundant algae growth to survive.

Common sea urchins:

Rock-boring Urchin (*Echinometra lucunter*) - these sea urchins can be reddish-brown to very dark brown with medium-length spines. Their bodies can reach up to 2 inches wide.

Mine Urchin (*Eucidaris tribuloides*) - these sea urchins can be reddish-orange to brown with a few thick, pointed spines. Their bodies can reach up to 2 inches wide.

Slate-pencil Urchin (*Heterocentrotus mammillatus*) - these sea urchins are red with thick blunt spines. Their bodies can reach up to 3 inches wide.

Long-spined Urchin (*Diadema antillarum*) - these sea urhins are black and have very long thin spins which produce a toxic venom. They are not good sea urchins for the aquarium. Their bodies can reach up to 3 inches wide.

Invertebrates

SHRIMP

(Phylum - Crustacea)

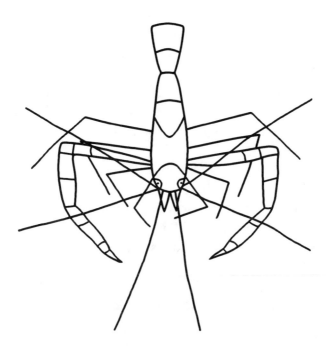

Banded-coral Shrimp

Physical characteristics

Shrimp are small, elongated crustaceans with walking legs and a muscular tail with a fin for rapid propulsion. They often have very long antenna that they use to help sense the environment. Some have very well developed claws. They

Invertebrates

can reach lengths of 1 to 3 inches in the aquarium and even longer in the wild.

Temperament

Most shrimps are peaceful and shy. The major exceptions to this are any of the Mantis Shrimp (order - Stomatopoda) which are extremely aggressive predators and should not be kept in an aquarium. Since shrimp are typically nocturnal, most of them will spend the day hiding among the rocks at the bottom. However, as they become more acclimated to aquarium life, some shrimp will be seen out during the day.

Feeding

Shrimp are scavengers by nature and consume bits of food they find on the ocean floor. In the aquarium they will eat fresh and frozen meaty foods.

Common shrimp:

Banded-coral Shrimp (*Stenopus hispidus*) - have alternating red and white bands over their entire bodies and well developed claws. These shrimp do not tolerate other members of their kind, so do not keep more than one unless you are sure that it is a mated pair. They can reach 2-3 inches in length.

Cleaner Shrimp (*Lysmata amboinensis*) - are translucent with a white stripe running the length of the dorsal side from head to tail. On each side of this white stripe is a red stripe that flows into the tail fin, which also has white dots. As the name suggests, Cleaner Shrimp will perform cleaning

Invertebrates

duties for many fish. They can reach 2-3 inches in length.

Blood Shrimp (*Lysmata debelius*) - are bright red with a few white dots on the dorsal side and on the lower half of their legs. They can reach 2-3 inches in length.

Peppermint Shrimp (*Rhynchocinetes uritai*) - are whitish to translucent in color with a wild matrix of red markings all over their bodies. They can reach 1 inch in length.

Anemone Shrimp (*Periclimenes brevicarpalis*) - are light reddish-orange in color with white spots along their bodies and a large white patch on their head. They can reach 1 inch in length.

Invertebrates

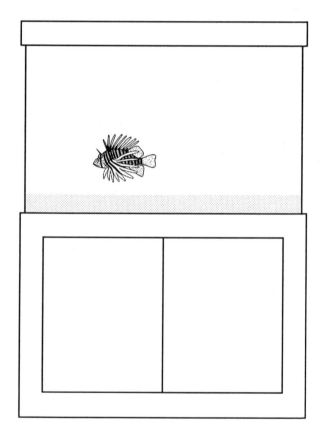

STARFISH

(Phylum - Echinodermata)

Comet Sea Star

Physical characteristics

Starfish have a small, flat, angular central body with five or more arms radiating outward. Their arms can vary from smooth to thorny and can be regenerated should one be lost due to injury or trauma. The brittle stars have segmented arms which allow them to readily shed pieces of an arm when threatened or attacked.

Temperament

Starfish are peaceful and spend their time stationary or slowly moving across the rocks or the sides of an aquarium.

Invertebrates

Feeding

Starfish with smooth legs are typically herbivores and scavengers and will eat algae and other bits of food in the aquarium. Starfish with knobby or thorny legs are typically flesh eaters that prey upon mollusks and other sessile invertebrates and can be fed pieces of fresh or frozen meaty foods.

Common starfish:

Comet Sea Star (*Linckia guildingii*) - these starfish are light brown and sometimes reddish. They can reach up to 9 inches in length.

Blue Starfish (*Linckia laevigata*) - are totally blue in color. They can reach 5-6 inches in length.

Spiny Brittle Star (*Ophiothrix spiculata*) - these starfish are brown, green, tan, orange, or yellow with long slender segmented arms. They can reach up to 12 inches in length.

Chapter 17

MARINE FISH DISEASES

In order to successfully maintain a salt water aquarium it is necessary to know some basic information about marine fish diseases and how to treat them. The most important aspects of maintaining good fish health are to provide a clean, healthy, stress free environment for them to live in and adequate nutrition to maintain and promote their metabolic functions. Once these conditions are met, the prospects of a fish becoming ill are greatly reduced.

Pathogens and parasites
All fish are host to large populations of pathogens and parasites which can be found on their skin as well as in their internal organs. A healthy fish lives in a balance with these pathogens and parasites so that all organisms exist in a beneficial relationship or at least in a non detrimental one. For example, some parasites may consume dead skin that the fish is constantly sloughing off, helping to keep the skin clean and healthy. Also, bacteria in the gut of the fish help digest food that has been eaten.

Bacteria
Bacteria are microscopic single-celled organisms with three primary shapes: rods (*Bacilli*), spheres (*Cocci*), or spirals (*Spirillum*). Other associated shapes are boomerang (*Vibrio*), long thin rods (*Flexibacter*) and short thin rods

(*Mycobacterium*). Bacteria are often assumed to be universally harmful; however, this is not true. Many different bacteria are beneficial, and life as we know it would not be possible without them. Some bacteria, on the other hand, can be quite detrimental to fish and are responsible for many different diseases.

Bacteria have the ability to reproduce rapidly, and thousands of generations can be created in a short period of time from a single bacterium. This rapid reproduction gives bacteria the ability to mutate into forms that are increasingly resistant to antibiotics. For bacteria, as in all life forms, survival of the fittest is a fact of life. The fittest in this case are the ones that can resist antibiotics. Therefore, antibiotics must be administered wisely and the instructions followed closely. A dose that is too weak or administered for too short a time will not kill all of the harmful bacteria and will eventually produce a more antibiotic resistant strain. If a biological filter is used with the aquarium, great care must also be taken when using antibiotics so as to not kill the *Nitrosomonas* and *Nitrobacter* bacteria. Common antibiotics used in the treatment of fish include: erythromycin, tetracycline, furazolidone, methylene blue, and malachite green.

Viruses
A virus is an extremely small organism that lives and reproduces within a living cell. Viruses are broken down into two groups depending on if they contain deoxyribonucleic acid (DNA) or ribonucleic acid (RNA). DNA is the molecule of heredity and RNA is the molecule of protein synthesis. When a virus is present in a living cell, it is able to rep-

Marine Fish Diseases

licate itself by commandeering the genetic material of the cell. In order to destroy the virus it is necessary to destroy the host cell. As such the only effective way to eliminate a virus is to isolate it and let the immune system attack it.

Some viral infections are harmless to an organism. Others are devastating. The best that can be hoped for is to isolate the fish, treat their symptoms, and give them every opportunity for their immune systems to prevail over the virus.

Fungus

A fungus is a plant-like organism that does not contain any chlorophyll and cannot perform photosynthesis. In order to survive it has to derive nutrition by consuming organic matter. Fungi reproduce by generating spores which are released into the environment where they may come into contact with living organisms. If the spores contact a healthy fish the fungus probably will not be able to survive. However, a fungus will readily manifest itself in a sick, weak, or injured fish. A fungus infection can be treated with antibiotics.

Parasites

A parasite is an organism that derives its nutrition from direct association with a host and often cannot survive without it. The host, on the other hand, typically suffers from the relationship and can readily survive without the parasite. Most parasites have complicated life cycles with many dramatic phases that may or may not be parasitic. Additionally, some parasites may associate for a time with an intermediate host such as a snail while other parasites do not. Some parasites are large and can be seen attached to the fish; however, many varieties are microscopic in size and can be found in the blood or internal organs.

Parasites are typically introduced into an aquarium by adding infected fish, plants, or snails. Once inside the aquarium, they can flourish either associated with a fish or an intermediate host. Proper maintenance and husbandry techniques, along with a thorough inspection and quarantine of all life forms that are introduced into the aquarium, go a long way toward avoiding and eliminating parasites. Once detected, though, most parasites can be eliminated by some or all of the following chemical treatments: antibiotics, copper, dimetridazole, metronidazole, and organophosphorus insecticides, such as metriphonate. Other measures include: thorough cleaning of the aquarium, elimination of intermediate hosts, raising the water temperature to around 90 degrees Fahrenheit for several hours (provided the fish can tolerate it), placing the fish in fresh water for several minutes, and physically removing the larger parasites. It is usually best to move the infected fish to a quarantine aquarium for treatment and to avoid spreading the parasites any further. However, be sure to treat the aquarium as well so that any parasites present there are eliminated.

Protozoans

A protozoa is a single-celled, microscopic organism that can be parasitic. Reproduction in a protozoa occurs by either asexual fusion or sexually. There are four kinds of protozoa: amoebas, ciliates, flagellates, and sporozoa. Amoe-

Marine Fish Diseases

bas have ever-changing shapes because of their jelly-like bodies that distend to provide locomotion. Ciliates have a large number of short hair-like projections that perform a wave-like action to achieve locomotion. Flagellates have one or more hair-like extremities for locomotion. Sporozoa are parasitic with complicated life cycles and no ability for locomotion in adults. Protozoans can be controlled with copper, freshwater baths, formalin, and malachite green.

Stress

As pointed out in Chapter 2, The Marine Environment, the conditions in the natural environment of a fish do not change rapidly. As a result, fish have poorly developed physiological mechanisms to effectively deal with stress and recover from it quickly. This means that stress has a very severe impact on the health of the fish and must be avoided as much as possible. The immune system of the fish helps keep the relationship between the fish and the pathogens and parasites in check so that it does not become ill or die. It is also to the benefit of the pathogens and parasites that the host fish does not die because they will lose their protection and nutrition source.

When a fish becomes stressed or injured, the immune system may not be able to keep the number of pathogens and parasites in check and the balance disappears. The result is a sick fish that could very well die if it is not cared for quickly and adequately. Stress can come from many sources such poor water quality, too high or too low water temperature, poor nutrition, unnecessary disturbance of the aquarium during cleaning, or by the introduction of new fish. Injury can be caused by such things as aggression from other fish, pumps and suction devices, or careless handling.

Foreign invaders

Another factor that can cause a fish to become ill is the introduction of new pathogens or parasites that the fish is not accustomed to. This is typically caused by adding unhealthy fish, unhealthy plants, unclean objects, or unclean food to the aquarium. These foreign invaders may be able to upset the balance and overwhelm the immune system of a fish causing it to become ill. Because of this, it is vitally important to make sure that new fish and plants are healthy before you introduce them into your aquarium. The best way to insure their health is to place the new fish and plants in a quarantine aquarium for a few days for observation before they are introduced into the display aquarium. Also, thoroughly clean any new decoration, hardware, or other objects before you put them into the aquarium. It is also very important to make sure that the food, especially the live food, is clean and untainted before you give it to the fish.

Nutrition

Fish also need proper nutrition. An improper diet leaves a fish with too little energy, as well as vitamin and mineral deficiencies, that weaken the fish's ability to protect against stress, injury, parasites, and pathogens. Once injured or ill, a malnourished fish will never recover and will eventually die.

Treatments

Whenever possible, it is best to remove the sick fish

to a quarantine aquarium for treatment. This makes it possible to administer a proper dosage of medication under controlled conditions. One of the best methods of removing a fish from the aquarium is to use a container, such as a wide mouth jar that is large enough to comfortably hold the fish. Place the container close to the fish and use nets to gently coax it toward and into the container. Then place the net over the mouth of the container and lift it out of the aquarium with the fish swimming inside. This method eliminates much of the stress that is caused by chasing a fish all over the aquarium trying to catch it in a net. It also avoids causing injury to the fish that can happen if a fin or other body part gets caught in the net.

Sometimes it is more convenient or even necessary to treat the entire aquarium. If this is the case, be sure that the treatment will not destroy or injure the *Nitrosomonas* and *Nitrobacter* bacteria in the biological filter. It is also best to remove any chemical filters such as activated carbon. If left in place, these filters can remove the medication from the water.

If you have any invertebrates, do not use copper to treat the aquarium. Most invertebrates are highly sensitive to copper and will die if exposed to it. There are several commercially available copper substitutes that are safe for invertebrates.

Taking care to provide a clean, stress-free environment with proper nutrition will go a very long way toward keeping your fish healthy. Unfortunately, in spite of our best efforts, our fish will sometimes become ill. The rest of this chapter discusses common marine fish diseases and illnesses, what causes them, and how they can be treated. The information on pathogens and parasites presented above, combined with the information below, should provide enough information to handle most sick marine fish. Once a determination has been made as to the nature of the illness, an informed decision can be made about the necessary treatment. Most aquarium shops have a wide variety of medicines and treatments available, and these items will provide even more specifics on what afflictions they can be used for and how they should be used.

One word of caution is in order at this point. It is possible for a human to become infected by handling a sick fish. To help protect yourself, wash your hands thoroughly with a disinfectant soap after handling the fish. For even more protection, wear latex or rubber gloves.

Black spots
Small black spots along the body of the fish are often caused by digenetic fluke parasites such as *Diplostomum*. Generally these parasites are harmless in low numbers and will eventually disappear because the marine aquarium is not a hospitable place for them. Larger infestations require intervention with an organophosphorus insecticide.

Bulging eyes
This condition can be caused by high ammonia or nitrite in the water resulting in a bacterial infection. Check water quality and if necessary perform extensive cleaning

Marine Fish Diseases

and maintenance on the aquarium to include several partial water changes to reduce the levels of ammonia and nitrite. If the condition does not improve, treat the fish with an antibacterial.

Cloudy eyes

Cloudy eyes can be caused by high ammonia or nitrite in the water resulting in a bacterial infection. Check water quality and if necessary perform extensive cleaning and maintenance on the aquarium and include several partial water changes to reduce the levels of ammonia and nitrite. It is also possible for this condition to be caused by poor nutrition resulting in vitamin deficiencies. Try altering the diet of the fish to include more protein.

Cloudy eyes can also be caused by digenetic fluke parasites. If a thorough cleaning of the aquarium and improved nutrition does not improve the condition, treat the fish with an antibacterial or anti-parasite chemical.

Cotton-like growths

Cotton-like growths can be the early stages of cotton wool disease which is also known as mouth fungus. This is a fungus-like growth around the mouth that is caused by the *Flexibacter* bacteria. In the early stages this infection appears as off-white marks on the mouth, body, or fins and eventually develops into white cotton-like growths around the mouth and reddish ulcers on the body and fins. Eventually a fungus-like growth around the mouth may develop. Since cotton wool disease is caused by the *Flexibacter* bacteria, an antibacterial treatment is called for.

Marine Fish Diseases

Emaciation

This condition is characterized by a shrunken belly or a body that looks like it is pinched just behind the head. A common cause of this is simple malnutrition, so pay special attention to the diet of the fish. Also, watch the fish during feedings to see if other, more aggressive fish are causing it to lose out in the competition for food. If so, special attention to the fish during feedings or possibly even removing it to a quarantine aquarium may be necessary to nurse it back to health.

If the fish is eating but the condition continues, it may be due to bacterial infection or possibly internal parasites. At this stage, it is best to remove the fish to a quarantine aquarium and treat with antibiotics.

Fin rot

Fin rot is characterized by ragged, split or missing fins. It can be triggered by a high level of stress such as poor water conditions, poor diet, overcrowding, etc. It is also possible that the missing fins are the result of other fish nipping at them. This is another form of stress that needs attention.

Fin rot can also be the result of a bacterial infection that has taken hold. If the stress-causing conditions mentioned above are corrected and the condition persists, an antibacterial treatment is called for.

Gasping

This condition is characterized by the fish sticking its mouth above the surface of the water as if it were gasping for

Marine Fish Diseases

air. The most common cause of this condition is poor water quality. This can be either a lack of oxygen, or an excess of carbon dioxide. Many oxygen and carbon dioxide problems can be solved by increased circulation. Remember that the surface water should be continually disturbed. Skimming the surface water as part of the filter input will help.

Gasping can also indicate an excess of ammonia and nitrite. These problems need to be corrected by performing maintenance on the filters and siphoning the organic debris and organic matter out of the aquarium followed by partial water changes.

Holes along the lateral line and on the head
Lateral line disease is characterized by ulceration of the lateral line and possibly part of the head. It is typically caused by stress or poor nutrition. Remedy these conditions by providing the kind of diet the fish requires and observing to see if it is losing out in the competition for food. If so, special attention is required to make sure the fish receives the amount of food it needs. It may be necessary to add vitamin C to the diet. Also determine if the fish is subject to any stress due to water conditions or aggressive neighbors.

Sometimes stray electrical currents can enter the water from circulation pumps or other sources. This can be corrected by grounding the water with a stainless steel wire connected to the ground of the electrical outlet. If you are not familiar with electrical circuits, have a qualified electrician make this connection for you.

Marine Fish Diseases

Jumping

Fish that make sudden dashes for the surface and even jump out of the aquarium may be suffering from too low pH or other water quality problems. Check the pH and adjust as necessary. Also check for proper circulation and surface disturbance as well as excess ammonia and nitrite levels and correct as necessary.

Rapid breathing

The most common cause of rapid breathing is poor water quality. Check the ammonia, and nitrite levels and correct by partial water changes if necessary. Also perform maintenance on the filters and siphon the organic debris out of the aquarium.

Red spots and patches

Red spots and patches at the base of the fins or on the body are usually caused by bacterial infections and should be treated with an antibiotic.

Slimy skin

This condition appears as a white to off white mucus like patch on the body of the fish. It can be caused by a monogenetic fluke which is living as a parasite on the fish's skin. This condition can be treated with a copper solution or by a freshwater dip of two to three minutes.

Swollen body

A swollen body that causes the scales to stick out is usually caused by a bacterial infection such as *Vibrio* and should be treated by an antibiotic.

Marine Fish Diseases

Ulcers and open sores

Ulcerations that first appear as small holes around the head, and often have excretions of mucus, are usually caused by the protozoan *Hexamita*. The common name for this condition is hole in the head disease and it can be treated with malachite green and antibiotics. A related condition to hole in the head disease is lateral line disease.

Velvet spots

This condition is characterized by very small yellow-gold spots on the body and fins. The fish may rub or scratch against rocks or the bottom substrate. This condition is known as velvet or coral fish disease and is caused by the parasitic dinoflagellate *Amyloodinium*. Treatment can be either a parasitic remedy, copper, or a two to three minute fresh water dip.

White spots

Fish with this condition have very small white spots on their body and fins. The fish may try to rub or scratch against rocks. This affliction is caused by protozoan parasites by the name of *Cryptocaryon irritans*. It is possible for white spot disease to develop as a result of recent stress to a fish which made it vulnerable to these parasites. Check to make sure that the water temperature has not fallen suddenly. Also check for other causes of stress in the tank and remedy any that are found. If these conditions are not the cause, then it should be treated with copper, fresh water baths, or other anti-parasitic chemicals.

Marine Fish Diseases

Chapter 18

INTRODUCTION TO MINI-REEFS

One of the most beautiful aquariums is the mini-reef. In a mini-reef the conditions are all optimized and maintained at an extremely high quality in an attempt to duplicate the conditions on a true coral reef. This makes it possible to nurture the more sensitive life forms such as macro algae and corals. As these life forms grow and flourish they create an even more balanced and natural environment.

As recently as the early 1970's, keeping coral alive in an aquarium was virtually unheard of and only a few true pioneers in the field had any success at all. Since then the level of knowledge regarding the physical conditions that corals require to live has advanced greatly. In addition, the equipments needed to duplicate these conditions have been developed and are readily available. Now, many serious aquarists are able to establish true mini reefs containing numerous kinds of coral. These corals are not just being kept alive, they are growing and flourishing!

Mini-reefs are much more difficult to keep than a fish-only aquarium, and a person should not attempt to start one unless thoroughly experienced, knowledgeable, and committed to the effort, and have adequate funds to do it correctly. If a mini-reef is not set up and maintained properly, the inhabitants will die needlessly.

Introduction To Mini-Reefs

Environmental concerns

This branch of the marine aquarium hobby is subject to some criticism from environmentalists. They claim that the hobby contributes to the continued demise of coral reefs and is environmentally unsound. In many areas it is even unlawful to harvest coral. The environmentalists' concerns are well noted and, if a mini-reef keeper is negligent, their concerns are well founded. So, it is imperative for anyone who attempts to start a mini-reef to do it right and not cause one animal to die prematurely. On the other hand, keeping mini-reefs has added greatly to the overall understanding of natural coral reefs - knowledge (such as the harmful effects of sedimentation and increased levels of nutrients caused by chemical pollution and run off from the land) that is used to help preserve the reefs and allow them to grow and flourish.

In the early days of mini-reef keeping, aquarists harvested their own coral and rocks containing reef inhabitants directly from a reef. This method is still being used today and has expanded with individuals and companies doing the collection for ultimate sale to the mini-reef aquarist. Some individuals and companies have even started to seed the sandy areas in the vicinity of a coral reef with rock. As time passes the various coral reef life forms start to inhabit these rocks and they are subsequently harvested for sale. This method of collecting is more environmentally sound. All of this rock, no matter how collected, is called "live rock." Some individuals and companies actually raise and reproduce many of these life forms for sale to mini-reef aquarists. In this regard, impact to the natural reefs is minimal, and the overall number of these organisms in the world actually increases.

Introduction To Mini-Reefs

There are two conditions that absolutely must be met to successfully maintain a mini-reef. First is lighting of the proper intensity and spectrum. Second is high quality filtration to maintain pristine water quality. These various conditions and some others are outlined in greater detail below.

Lights

As discussed in Chapter 9, Lights, animals such as corals and giant clams are symbiotic hosts to algae cells called *Zooxanthellae* which perform photosynthesis and produce carbohydrates to nourish the host. The chlorophyll in the *Zooxanthellae* absorb sunlight in the 400 to 450 and 600 to 650 nanometer wavelength range. These wavelengths equate to the violet-blue and orange-red frequencies, respectively. In addition, *Zooxanthellae* require a high intensity of light to carry out photosynthesis. Normal florescent and incandescent light bulbs do not provide enough light in the proper frequencies to sustain life in the *Zooxanthellae*. Therefore, specialized florescent and metal halide light bulbs have been developed that mimic sunlight in intensity and frequency. They are expensive and many are needed, and a mini-reef can not be sustained without them.

Filtration

The water found in a mini-reef is of extremely high quality. The levels of pollutants, organic waste, and toxins are extremely low providing a clean, healthy environment. Additionally, the clarity of the water is extremely high allowing the maximum amount of light to penetrate. The only way to achieve this high water quality is with extensive biological filtration, and the primary equipment of choice is a

Introduction To Mini-Reefs

wet/dry filter and a protein skimmer. Attempting to sustain corals with more conventional filter systems is an invitation for disaster.

Other conditions

All of the other conditions discussed earlier in this book such as: robust circulation, proper temperature, thin substrate, high levels of maintenance, etc., are even more vital in a mini-reef. The mini-reef operates in a delicate environmental balance and maintaining the aquarium and all of the electrical and mechanical equipment in good condition is absolutely required. There are no short cuts with a mini-reef.

Feeding

The nutritional requirements of corals and other mini-reef animals are even more demanding than they are for fish. Large anemones are easy to feed and are given small chunks of fish meat about once a week. Beyond the nutrition provided by *Zooxanthellae*, filter feeders such as clams and corals also require supplements of micro nutrients. However, with the efficient filtration system, most micro nutrients are quickly removed from the aquarium environment much to the detriment of these animals. So, it is often necessary to stop filtration for a short period of time so that the corals and other animals get their full measure of these nutrients.

It should be obvious that maintaining a healthy mini-reef is a much greater undertaking than a fish-only aquarium. If you are seriously interested in setting up a mini-reef, thoroughly research and study all aspects of the subject, improve and refine your aquarium keeping skills, and save money for

Introduction To Mini-Reefs

the required investments. If you do everything right you will be rewarded with a beautiful mini-reef. As you watch your mini-reef grow and flourish you will derive great satisfaction and gain deeper insights into life on this earth.

Introduction To Mini-Reefs

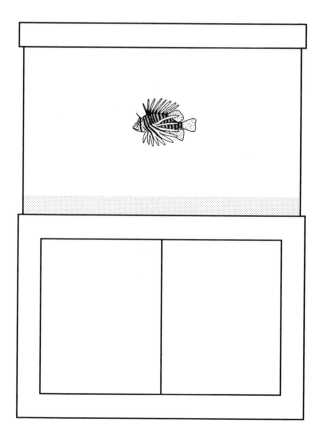

INDEX

Abudefduf cyaneus: 117
Abudefduf saxatilis: 117
Acanthuridae: 147
Acanthurus achilles: 149
Acanthurus coeruleus: 148
Acanthurus leucosternon: 149
Acanthurus lineatus: 149
Acanthurus triostegus: 149
Achilles Tang: 149
Algae: 5, 57, 58, 78, 79, 81, 83, 84, 87, 88, 92, 93, 98, 106, 120, 134, 136, 148, 166, 172, 189
Algae, blooms: 58, 92, 93
Algae, brown: 22
Algae, macro: 160, 187
Alkalinity: 86
Ammonia: 32, 47-49, 75, 77, 86, 90, 180-184
Amoebas: 176, 177
Amphiprion ephippium: 112, 113
Amphiprion frenatus: 112, 113
Amphiprion ocellaris: 112
Amyloodinium: 185
Anemonefish: 115
Anemones: 58, 106, 111, 112, 160
Anemone Shrimp: 169
Angelfish: 97-99
Antibiotics: 174-276, 181, 182, 184, 185
Apogonidae: 109
Apogon maculatus: 110

Arc Eye Hawkfish: 125, 126
Arrow Crab: 162
Artemia salina: 80
Aspidontus taeniatus: 104
Bacilli: 173
Bacteria: 39, 41, 52, 67, 68, 80, 82, 93, 173, 174, 180-182, 184
Balistes vetula: 152
Balistidae: 119, 151
Balistoides conspicillum: 152, 153
Banana Wrasse: 157
Banded Butterflyfish: 107
Banded-coral Shrimp: 167, 168
Batfish: 101, 102
Bicolor Blenny: 103, 104
Birdmouth Wrasse: 157
Blue Tang: 148
Black-banded Butterflyfish: 107
Black Cap Gramma: 124
Black-saddled Puffer: 143, 144
Black-tailed Damselfish: 116
Black Triggerfish: 153
Blennidae: 103
Blennies: 103, 104, 121, 156
Blood Shrimp: 169
Bloodworms: 82
Blue Chromis: 117
Blue Damsel: 117
Blue Starfish: 172
Blue-striped Butterflyfish: 107
Blue Surgeon: 149

Index

Brine shrimp: 80-83, 102, 106, 120, 128, 130, 134, 146, 156
Bodianus pulchellus: 157
Bodianus rufus: 157
Broccoli: 83
Bubbles: 37, 38, 43-45, 50, 74, 81
Butterflyfish: 105-107
Calcium: 86
Callionymidae: 133
Canthigaster solandri: 144
Canthigaster valentini: 144
Carbon, activated: 40, 43, 46, 47, 73, 91, 179
Cardinalfish: 109, 110
Catalina Goby: 122
Centropyge bispinous: 98
Centropyge loriculus: 98
Chaetodon frembli: 107
Chaetodon lunula: 107
Chaetodon melannotus: 107
Chaetodon striatus: 107
Chaetodontidae: 105
Chemicals, salt water: 27, 28
Chemlon rostratus: 106, 107
Chillers: 63-66
Chilomycterus schoepfi: 140
Chironomidae: 82
Chlorophyll: 57, 175, 189
Chromis caerulea: 117
Chromis cyanea: 117
Chromis xanthurus: 117
Ciliates: 176, 177
Circulation, tank: 35, 36, 38, 42, 43, 50, 64, 74, 81, 82, 183, 190
Circulation, how much: 35, 36
Circulation, surface: 35, 36, 38, 40, 42, 53, 54
Cirrhilabrus rubriventralis: 157
Cirrhitidae: 125
Clams: 35, 58, 83, 84, 128, 160, 189, 190
Cleaner Shrimp: 168, 169
Cleaner Wrasse: 104, 155, 156
Clownfish: 111-113
Clown Surgeon: 149
Clown Wrasse: 156
Cocci: 173
Comet Sea Star: 171, 172
Common Porcupinefish: 140
Convict Tang: 149
Copper: 86, 176, 177, 179, 184, 185
Copper-band Butterflyfish: 105-107
Coral: 5, 23-25, 58, 59, 63, 78, 98, 105-107, 110, 120, 156, 160, 187-190
Coral Beauty: 98
Coral fish disease: 185
Coris gaimardi: 156
Cotton wool disease: 181
Crabs: 84, 138, 161, 162
Crustacea: 161, 163, 167
Crustaceans: 121, 134, 136, 138, 140, 141, 144, 156, 163, 167
Cryptocaryon irritans: 185
Ctenochaetus strigosus: 149
Cuban Hogfish: 157
Damselfish: 111, 115-117
Dardanus megistos: 162
Dascyllus aruanus: 116
Dascyllus melanurus: 116
Dascyllus trimaculatus: 116
Dendrochirus brachypterus: 131
Density: 29
Deoxyribonucleic acid: 174
Diadema antillarum: 166

Index

Dimetridazole: 176
Dinoflagellate: 185
Diodon holacanthus: 140
Diodon hystrix: 140
Diodontidae: 139
Diplostomum: 180
DLS: 52
DNA: 174
Domino Damsel: 115-117
Dragonets: 133
Dwarf Parrot Wrasse: 157
Echnida nebulosa: 138
Echinodermata: 165, 171
Echinometra lucunter: 166
Ecsenius bicolor: 104
Ecsenius midas: 104
Electrical currents: 183
Emaciation: 182
Emperor Angelfish: 99
Enchytraeid: 82
Enoplometopus occidentalis: 164
Erythomycin: 174
Eucidaris tribuloides: 166
Evaporation: 33, 92
Eye, false: 106, 107
Eyes, bulging: 180, 181
Eyes, cloudy: 181
Fairy basslet: 123
False Cleanerfish: 104, 156
Fantail Filefish: 120
Fiddler Crab: 161
Filefish: 119, 120
Filter, activated carbon: 40, 43, 46, 47, 73, 91
Filter, biological media: 52, 73
Filter, bubble: 43
Filter, carbon: 71
Filter, chemical: 46, 53, 93, 179

Filter, circulation: 36, 37
Filter, diatomaceous earth: 45
Filter, double layer spiral: 52, 73
Filter, external canister: 42, 43, 45, 72, 77, 90
Filter, external tank: 40-43, 45, 54, 72, 77, 90
Filter, polyester floss: 40-43, 45, 46, 72, 73, 90, 91
Filter, molecular adsorption: 46-48
Filter, polyurethane foam: 40, 73, 90, 91
Filter, protein skimmer: 44-46, 53, 73, 78
Filter, trickle: 52
Filter, undergravel: 19, 50, 51, 55, 70, 78
Filter, wet/dry: 15, 42, 51-55, 72, 73, 78, 90, 190
Filtration, biological: 6, 21, 39, 41, 42, 47, 49-52, 90, 174, 179, 190
Filtration, chemical: 6, 46
Filtration, mechanical: 6, 39, 40, 42, 45-47, 49, 50, 53
Fin, anal: 96, 130, 147, 153
Fin, caudal: 96, 99, 104, 107, 117, 130, 137, 145, 147, 155
Fin, dorsal: 96, 106, 107, 109, 110, 116, 117, 119, 126, 131, 135, 137, 147, 149, 151, 153
Fin, pectoral: 96, 125, 129, 131, 137, 155
Fin, pelvic: 96, 130
Fin problems: 181, 184, 185
Fin rot: 182
Fin, ventral: 96, 117
Fish, adding: 75, 76
Fish, anatomy: 95

Index

Fish, feeding: 79-84
Fish, number of: 12, 13, 77, 78
Flagellates: 173, 181
Flame Angelfish: 97, 98
Flamefish: 110
Flash-back Gramma: 141, 142
Flexibacter: 173, 181
Florida Seahorse: 145, 146
Flukes: 181, 184
Food, flake: 83, 110
Food, from kitchen: 83, 84
Food, frozen: 82, 83, 106, 112, 116, 122, 123, 126, 130, 134, 141, 146, 156, 162, 164, 168, 172
Food, how much: 84
Food, live: 79-81, 110, 112, 116, 122, 123, 126, 130, 134, 141, 144, 146, 178
Food, meaty: 98, 112, 126, 128, 130, 138, 140, 144, 162, 164, 168, 172
Food, vegetable: 112, 148, 156
Formalin: 177
French Angelfish: 99
Freshwater dips: 176, 184, 185
Fungus: 67, 175, 181
Furizolidone: 174
Gasping: 182
Gills: 96, 97, 137, 156
Gobies: 121, 122
Gobiidae: 121
Gobiodon citrinus: 122
Gobiodon okinawae: 122
Gomphosus caeruleus: 157
Gramma loreto: 124
Gramma melacara: 124
Grammas: 123, 124, 141
Grammidae: 123, 141

Green Chromis: 117
Green Parrotfish: 158
Green Parrot Wrasse: 158
Growths, cotton like: 181
Halichoeres chrysus: 157
Hawkfish: 125, 126
Heaters: 6, 63, 64, 71
Hermit Crabs: 161, 162
Heterocentrotus mammillatus: 166
Hexamita: 185
Hippocampus erectus: 146
Hippocampus kuda: 146
Holacanthus ciliaris: 98
Holacanthus tricolor: 98
Hole in the head disease: 185
Hydrometer: 30, 31
Immune system: 175, 177, 178
Intermediate hosts: 175, 176
Jawfish: 127, 128
Jumping: 183
Kelp: 83
Kole Tang: 149
Krill: 83
Labridae: 155
Labroides dimidiatus: 156
Lagoon Triggerfish: 153
Lateral line: 96, 183
Lateral line disease:
Lemon Goby: 122
Lettuce: 83
Lights: 6, 15, 57-60, 73, 91, 92, 189
Light, fluorescent: 59, 60, 189
Light frequency: 58, 189
Light, incandescent: 59, 189
Light, intensity: 60, 189
Light, metal halide: 59, 189
Light, reflectors: 60

Index

Light, spectrum: 6, 58-60
Light, sunlight: 5, 6, 57, 58, 92, 93
Linckia guildingii: 172
Linckia laevigata: 172
Lionfish: 84, 129-131
Lobsters: 163, 164
Long-nosed Filefish: 119, 120
Long-nosed Hawkfish: 126
Long-spined Porcupinefish: 140
Long-spined Urchin: 166
Lysmata amboinensis: 168
Lysmata debelius: 169
Lythrypnus dalli: 122
Malachite green: 174, 177, 185
Mandarinfish: 133, 134
Mantis Shrimp: 168
Methyl blue: 174
Metriphonate: 176
Metronidazole: 176
Midas Blenny: 104
Mine Urchin: 166
Mollusks: 156
Monocanthidae: 119
Moorish Idol: 135, 136
Moray Eels: 137, 138
Mouth fungus: 181
Muraenidae: 137
Mycobacterium: 173
Neocirrhites armatus: 126
Neon-back Gramma: 142
Nitrate: 32, 48, 49, 75, 86, 90
Nitrite: 32, 48, 49, 75, 77, 86, 90, 180, 181, 183, 184
Nitrogen: 47
Nitrogen cycle: 48, 49, 75, 77, 115
Nitrosomonas: 48-51, 77, 174, 179
Nitrobacter: 48-51, 77, 174, 179
Nutrition: 3, 173, 175, 177-179, 181-183, 190

Odonus niger: 153
Operculum: 96
Ophiothrix spiculata: 172
Opistognathidae: 127
Opistognathus aurifrons: 128
Organic debris: 5, 6, 20-24, 35, 39, 44-47, 53, 58, 68, 88-90, 92, 183, 184, 188, 189
Organic nutrients: 58, 92, 93
Overflow box: 54, 73
Oxycirrhites typus: 126
Oxymonacanthus longirostris: 120
Ozone: 67
Pajama Cardinalfish: 109, 110
Panulirus versicolor: 164
Paracanthurus hepatus: 149
Paracirrhites arcatus: 126
Parasites: 77, 156, 173, 175-182, 184, 185
Parrot fish: 22, 23
Pathogens: 173, 177-179
Pepermint Shrimp: 169
Percula Clown: 111, 112
Periclimenes brevicarpalis: 169
Pervagor spilosoma: 120
Pterois antennata: 130
Pterois radiata: 130, 131
Pterois volitans: 130
Petrosciretes temmincki: 104
PH: 3, 31, 32, 75, 86, 184
Phosphate: 47, 86, 93
Photosynthesis: 58, 59, 175, 189
Picasso Trigger: 151, 152
Pigmy basslets: 123
Plankton: 106, 146
Platacidae: 101
Platax orbicularis: 102
Pomacanthidae: 97

Index

Pomacanthus imperator: 99
Pomacanthus paru: 99
Pomacentridae: 111, 115
Porcupinefish: 139, 140, 143
Powder Blue Surgeon: 149
Power head: 37, 50, 51, 67, 73
Protein skimmer: 44-46, 53, 73, 77
Protozoa: 176, 177, 184, 185
Pseudochromidae: 123, 141, 142
Pseudochromis: 141, 142
Pseudochromis diadema: 142
Pseudochromis dutoiti: 142
Pseudochromis porphyreus: 142
Psychedelic Fish: 134
Puffers: 143, 144
Pump, air: 37, 38, 44, 81, 82
Pump, water: 36, 37, 40-42, 44, 45, 50, 53, 55, 56, 65, 67, 73, 74, 178, 183
Purple Spiny Lobster: 163, 164
Pygmy basslets: 141
Quarantine: 76, 176, 178, 179, 182
Queen Angelfish: 98
Queen Trigger: 152
Racoon Butterflyfish: 107
Rapid breathing: 184
Rectangular Triggerfish: 153
Red Dwarf Lobster: 164
Red Hermit Crab: 161, 162
Red-tailed Surgeon: 149
Regal Tang: 149
Rhinecanthus aculeatus: 152
Rhinecanthus rectangulus: 153
Rhynchocinetes uritai: 169
Ribonucleic acid: 174
RNA: 174
Rock Beauty: 98
Rock-boring Urchin: 165, 166

Royal Gramma: 123, 124
Sailfin Tang: 148
Salinity: 3, 28-31, 33, 71, 75, 81, 90, 92
Saltwater mix: 32, 33, 71, 81, 89, 90
Salt water, natural: 32
Sand: 22, 88, 89
Sand, crushed coral: 22, 23, 56, 156
Sand - see Substrate
Scarlet Hawkfish: 126
Scooter Blenny: 104
Scorpaenidae: 129
Scorpionfish: 130
Seahorses: 145, 146
Sea urchins: 152, 165, 166
Sergeant Major: 117
Sharp-nosed Puffer: 144
Shrimp: 83, 167-169
Siphon: 24, 25, 39, 40, 44, 52, 55, 71, 88, 90, 183, 184
Siphon, reverse: 55, 56
Siphon, starting: 72
Skimmer box: 53-55
Skimmer, protein:
Slate-pencil Urchin: 166
Slimy skin: 184
Snails: 176
Snowflake Moray: 137, 138
Spanish Hogfish: 157
Specific gravity: 28-31
Sphaeramia nematopterus: 110
Spiny Boxfish: 139, 140
Spiny Brittle Star: 172
Spirillum: 173
Sponges: 35, 98, 106
Sporozoa: 176, 177
Spots, black: 180

Index

Spots, red: 184
Spots, velvet: 185
Spots, white: 185
Squid: 83, 84, 128
Stands: 16-18, 69, 70, 91
Starfish: 171, 172
Stomatopoda: 168
Strawberry Gramma: 142
Stenopus hispidus: 168
Stenorhynchus seticornis: 162
Stress: 1, 3, 5, 76, 84, 90, 106, 139, 143, 173, 177-179, 182, 183, 185
Substrate, cleaning: 88, 89
Substrate, crushed coral: 22, 23, 156
Substrate, sand: 22
Substrate, thickness: 20-22, 70, 128, 190
Surge makers: 67
Surgeons: 147-150
Swollen body: 184
Synchiropus picturatus: 134
Synchiropus splendidus: 134
Syngnathidae: 145, 146
Tangs: 79, 147-150
Tanks, acrylic: 7, 8-10, 12, 13, 69, 87
Tanks, glass: 7-9, 12, 69, 87
Tanks, size: 10-13
Temperature: 3, 6, 29, 30, 63-65, 75, 76, 81, 90, 176, 177, 185, 190
Testing, water: 70, 77, 86, 87
Tetracycline: 174
Thalassoma lunare: 158
Thermometer: 30
Tomato Clown: 112, 113
Trace elements: 28, 33, 90
Triggerfish: 119, 151-153

Turkeyfish: 131
Tubifex worms: 82
Ulcers: 184
Ultraviolet sterilizers: 67, 68
Velvet: 185
Vibrio: 73, 184
Viruses: 67, 174, 175
Vitamins: 178, 181, 183
Water, partial changes: 89, 90, 180, 181, 183, 184
Water, testing: 32, 70, 77, 86, 87
Wave makers: 67
White-fin Lionfish: 130, 131
White-tailed Damselfish: 116
White worms: 82
Wrasses: 155-158
Yellow Goby: 121, 122
Yellow-headed Jawfish: 127, 128
Yellow Seahorse: 146
Yellow Tang: 147-149
Yellow-tailed Damselfish: 117
Zanclidae: 135
Zanclus canescens: 135
Zebrasoma flavescens: 148
Zebrasoma veliferum: 148
Zooxanthellae: 57-60, 189, 190

A Living Jewel

ABOUT THE AUTHOR

Robert L. Fuqua was born in south central Kansas in October 1949 and grew up there learning the mid-western values and work ethic. In 1971 he graduated from Kansas State University with a B.S. degree in Mechanical Engineering. The next four years found him in the U.S. Air Force, which brought him to Maryland where he started his career as an engineer. A lifelong goal was finally realized in 1977, when he became a certified SCUBA diver. Between the travelling required by his job and the holidays he has taken, he has been fortunate enough to dive and snorkel all over the world. He also worked as a volunteer diver at the National Aquarium in Baltimore for five years and eventually became the Sunday Dive Captain.

He started learning about aquariums and fish as a young boy and his interest has steadily grown throughout his life. He acquired his first saltwater aquarium in 1979 after years of keeping freshwater aquariums. During a four-year job assignment in Hawaii from 1987 to 1991 he started getting interested in mini-reefs and learned the basics with two 50-gallon aquariums. Upon returning to Maryland, he established a 150-gallon mini-reef that is home to a wide variety of hard and soft corals, macro algaes, two clams, several fish and numerous other coral reef inhabitants.

A Living Jewel

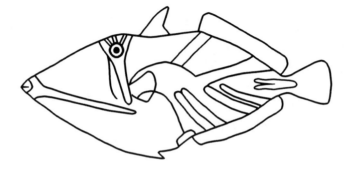

Notes

Notes

Notes

Notes

A Living Jewel

ORDER FORM

Please send _____ additional copies of *A Living Jewel* to:

Name:

Address:

City: State: Zip:

Each book: 10.00
Shipping each book   1.50

Total for each book: 11.50

Maryland residents please add 5% sales tax.

Send a check or money order for the total amount to:

DRAGONFLY PRODUCTIONS
4505 Linthicum Road
Dayton, Md. 21036

Please allow 3-4 weeks for delivery.

THANK YOU

A Living Jewel

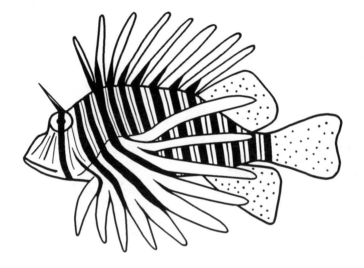